PROTECT YOUR ELDERLY PARENTS:
BECOME YOUR PARENTS' GUARDIAN OR TRUSTEE

PROTECT YOUR ELDERLY PARENTS: BECOME YOUR PARENTS' GUARDIAN OR TRUSTEE

Lynne Butler, Lawyer

Self-Counsel Press
(a division of)
International Self-Counsel Press Ltd.
Canada   USA

Self-Counsel Press acknowledges the financial support of the Government of Canada through the Book Publishing Industry Development Program (BPIDP) for our publishing activities.

Printed in Canada.

First edition: 2008

Library and Archives Canada Cataloguing in Publication

Butler, Lynne
    Protect your elderly parents / Lynne Butler.

    ISBN 978-1-55180-802-4

    1. Aging parents—Legal status, laws, etc.—Canada. 2. Aging parents—Care—Canada.
    3. Adult children of aging parents—Canada—Family relationships. I. Title.
    HQ1063.6.B88 2008   346.7101'3   C2007-907232-1

ANCIENT FOREST FRIENDLY Self-Counsel Press is committed to protecting the environment and to the responsible use of natural resources. We are acting on this commitment by working with suppliers and printers to phase out our use of paper produced from ancient forests. This book is one step toward that goal. It is printed on 100 percent ancient-forest-free paper (100 percent post-consumer recycled), processed chlorine- and acid-free.

Self-Counsel Press
(a division of)
International Self-Counsel Press Ltd.

1481 Charlotte Road
North Vancouver, BC V7J 1H1
Canada

1704 North State Street
Bellingham, WA 98225
USA

CONTENTS

TABLES

SAMPLES

NOTICE

INTRODUCTION

More and more Canadians are currently facing the challenge of looking after elderly parents or relatives who are losing the ability to look after themselves. As Canada's baby boomers get older, the number of individuals requiring assistance will continue to increase. An elderly person might lose the ability to look after himself or herself because of the onset of Alzheimer's disease, vascular dementia, injury, brain tumour, or for many other reasons.

Often it is the elderly person's children who are willing and able to offer a shoulder to lean on. The kind of help needed can range from depositing the monthly pension cheque in the bank to cooking meals. Again, it is often the elderly person's children who know that daily tasks have become a problem for the person. Whether it is loss of ability to make personal- and health-care decisions or loss of ability to make financial decisions, the loss of a

person's ability to make reasonable decisions and choices is referred to as the *loss of capacity*.

Once the children of an elderly person have come forward with a willingness to help, they may find that helping out is not as simple as they might have hoped. For example, a person who intends to help his or her elderly mother with her banking or tax returns may be told that they are not entitled to receive information or to sign documents regarding the mother, or that they do not have the authority to speak for her. If he or she is trying to register the mother for a long-term care facility or medical procedure, they may be told that they do not have the proper authority to deal with these things. This is the point where legal documents that appoint a guardian or trustee must be considered.

If the aging relative has already signed papers that appoint someone to make decisions for him or her after capacity is lost, it is possible that no further legal steps need to be taken at that time. If the elderly person has already put a valid power of attorney and a Health Care Directive into place, the family members will already be in a position to legally help their parent. However, not everyone has signed such papers. In fact, the majority of elderly Canadians have not done so.

This book will talk about what to do if those papers have not been signed but your elderly relative needs help. In many cases, once it becomes apparent that an aging relative is unable to look after himself or herself, the family is advised to have a guardian and/or trustee appointed on behalf of that relative. Sometimes this suggestion comes from a bank or a hospital that deals with the aging relative. Sometimes it is suggested by the relative's doctor, lawyer, or financial advisor. If the suggestion is followed by the family, it usually involves someone asking the court to appoint him or her as guardian or trustee for the aging relative. The idea of undertaking the court process can be intimidating. It can even be overwhelming. Many people wonder if the court process is too costly, time consuming, or complicated and, as a result, put off the decision for too long, leaving the elderly relative with nobody legally able to help him or her.

Even if there are people willing to make a court application, most of them have only a passing familiarity with guardianship and trusteeship and do not necessarily know what they are getting into. Their only knowledge may be snippets of information passed on by friends who are looking after relatives of their own. In some parts of Canada, there is not much legal information available for the public about guardianship and trusteeship. This book will explore the roles of guardian and trustee in some detail. It will discuss the powers of guardians and trustees as well as the restrictions placed on them in order to give as full a picture as possible of the role you are considering.

Helping aging individuals can be a balancing act. The dependent adults have to be protected from unscrupulous persons, while at the same time encouraged to maintain dignity and independence for as long as they can safely do so. We all know of older people who have been taken advantage of by deceitful people and none of us want that to happen to our own older relatives. At the same time, we do not want to take away their right to live their own lives as they wish.

Chapter 3 discusses alternatives to the court process. Every person considering guardianship or trusteeship should consider the suggestions contained in that chapter prior to making a court application. Some readers may find that they can achieve their goal of protecting their parents without resorting to the courts. This is where you should start, as the general approach taken by the Canadian courts is that every adult is presumed to be able to look after his or her own affairs unless it is proven that he or she cannot. The courts also assume that you have not rushed into a court application but that you have fully considered all of the alternatives before choosing a court application as the best choice available.

If, however, none of the alternatives presented are going to be of help in your particular situation, this book will show you how to make that first court application to get appointed, as well as how to make an application for a review of an existing court order.

Having a guardian and trustee appointed can bring peace of mind to family members who are not sure which of them should be looking after their parents, or who are worried about their elderly relatives being vulnerable to strangers and family members alike. Putting one person in charge may also help cut down on disputes among family members who cannot agree on how matters should be dealt with. Having one person put in charge will also give stability to the elderly relative, as he or she will know with whom they should be discussing their plans.

Reading this book cannot take the place of getting legal advice from an experienced lawyer who is familiar with the facts of your particular case. The information and advice in this book are necessarily general. Most readers will find the information, ideas, and forms they need in this book. However, if you find that the application process or the accounting responsibilities are too much to manage on your own, it is better to consult a lawyer for help than to leave your older relative without a guardian or trustee.

The concepts of guardianship and trusteeship are similar all across Canada, so you will find that almost all of the information in this book applies to you no matter where you live in Canada. Where there is important information that applies only to one province or territory, that information is presented in this book in a way that clearly shows it is only applicable to that part of the country.

The forms to be filed at the court for each province and territory are different because they are made by provincial or territorial laws, not federal laws. The approaches taken by various provinces and territories are astonishingly different from each other, depending partly on how recently the province or territory in

question has updated its dependent adult laws. Those that have more recently been updated tend to be the easiest to use without the assistance of a lawyer. Once you have decided which application you want to make (guardianship, trusteeship, or both) you will find the checklist on the CD that applies to your province or territory, which lists the forms you will need to prepare.

The main focus of this book is the protection of elderly parents. However, the process for being appointed described in this book is the same process that is used to appoint a guardian and trustee for any adult who needs one, regardless of the reason for the need. For example, a man in his 30s might need a guardian if he is in a motorcycle accident and suffers a brain injury that incapacitates him. The court application process would be identical, even though the reason for the application was very different.

The focus of this book is not about rescuing adults who have been abused or neglected. All jurisdictions across Canada have laws in place that deal with protection of adults of all ages who are subject to physical abuse, sexual abuse, mental cruelty, or neglect in the place that they live. The laws and procedures discussed in this book are separate from those laws. If you wish to assist or rescue an elderly person whom you believe to be in distress of any kind, you are encouraged to contact your local police, social services agency, or elder abuse agency.

Once you have been successful in asking the court to appoint you as guardian and/or trustee, you may refer to this book again for information about what is involved in court reviews and passing of accounts. The book also covers what happens when the dependent adult dies or the guardian and/or trustee dies.

THE DIFFERENCE BETWEEN A GUARDIAN AND TRUSTEE

1. Understanding the Difference between a Guardian and Trustee

If you are reading this book, you are most likely in the following situation:

- It has become clear to you that an elderly parent needs assistance of some kind, whether it is with personal- and/or health- care matters, financial matters, or both personal and financial matters.

- None of the alternatives such as home care, power of attorney, or Health Care Directives discussed in Chapter 3 are suitable for the elderly relative in question.

- You have decided that the court system, though it is a last resort, is the best choice right now for the elderly relative in question.

This chapter will help you clarify the difference between a guardian and trustee. A person may apply to the court to be appointed as a guardian or a trustee, or both. This book will consider guardianship and trusteeship to be two different roles, even though one person can, and often does, do both jobs at once. If you are applying for both, you only have to make one application. Chapter 2 will help you understand which role is suitable for your elderly relative.

The main difference between guardianship and trusteeship lies in the type of decisions that must be made by the person who is appointed. The type of decisions that need to be made will depend on the unique situation and needs of the person who is being protected. For example, some elderly adults can live on their own reasonably well but cannot manage their finances, while others are just the opposite. The elderly person being protected will be referred to as a "dependent adult" in this book because he or she is an adult who is now becoming dependent on others for assistance.

In provincial and territorial statutes, the person who is in need of assistance is referred to by different names. In order to make it easier for you to read and understand your own local laws, use Table 1 to determine what such a person is properly called in your province or territory.

You will note that in most cases, the terms used to describe an adult who needs assistance with decision making refer to the concept of being incapable or incapacitated. As more and more parts of Canada modernize their laws dealing with assisting incapacitated adults, the language used in those laws also becomes more up-to-date. By and large, Canada has done away with language that referred to incapacitated adults in somewhat derogatory terms, though one or two provinces have yet to reform their laws. The modern-day laws recognize that adults who are losing or have lost their capacity should be treated with respect and dignity.

Guardianship and trusteeship should not be undertaken lightly. Keep in mind that Canada's Charter of Rights ensures each person the right to life, liberty, and security of the person. You must understand that by asking a court to appoint you as someone else's guardian or trustee, you are asking it to take away another person's right to run his or her own affairs. For this reason, you are encouraged to ask the court only for the powers you

Table 1
NAME OF PERSON IN NEED OF ASSISTANCE BY PROVINCE AND TERRITORY

Province or Territory	Name of Person in Need of Assistance
Alberta	Dependent adult
British Columbia	Patient
Manitoba	Incompetent person
New Brunswick	Mentally incompetent person
Newfoundland and Labrador	Mentally disabled person
Northwest Territories	Represented person
Nova Scotia	Mentally incompetent person
Nunavut	Represented person
Ontario	Incapable person
Prince Edward Island	Incompetent person
Saskatchewan	Incapable adult
Yukon	Incapable adult

need to assist the dependent adult, and no more. Asking for more is at best interference and at worst, an infringement on another person's rights.

The general attitude that you should take when considering guardianship and trusteeship is that dependent adults should be encouraged to remain as independent as possible for as long as safely possible. Only the help that is requested or needed by a dependent adult should be given. Taking away an individual's independence can be an indignity to the person that is in some cases avoidable. Some elderly people feel angry and violated if unwanted assistance is imposed on them by well-intentioned family members who have too heavy a hand. Guardians and trustees should tread as lightly as possible while giving the assistance that is needed.

Guardianship and trusteeship laws were created for one purpose only, which is to assist a dependent adult. All of the provincial and territorial statutes give the courts the discretion to appoint a guardian and trustee if the court believes it to be beneficial to the dependent adult.

Provincial and territorial legislatures are also doing away with laws that allow a guardian or trustee to have absolute and full control of a person and his or her health care and finances once incapacity has been shown. The more forward-thinking provinces and territories recognize that individuals suffering from loss of capacity do not necessarily need every single area of responsibility taken from them. This is where the difference between guardianship and trusteeship comes in. It is simply a matter of time until all areas of Canada are fully modernized in this way.

1.1 Guardianship

A guardian deals with decisions of a personal nature. This includes health-related decisions such as whether the dependent adult should have a particular surgical operation, take specific medication, or see a doctor. It usually also extends to other personal decisions such as where the dependent adult will live and even small, day-to-day decisions such as what the dependent adult will eat and what he or she will wear. The guardian is the person who would make those decisions on behalf of the dependent adult. As each individual dependent adult is different, so will the decisions needed to be made by each guardian. The general idea is to assist the dependent adult where necessary while allowing him or her to live as independently as possible.

A guardian does not make decisions relating to money, bills, investments, finances, or property. A guardian has no authority to sell or rent a dependent adult's house, pay his or her bills, receive an inheritance on his or her behalf, or invest the dependent person's savings.

The Guardianship and Trusteeship Act of the Northwest Territories, though it only applies to Northwest Territories and Nunavut, contains valuable guidance for anyone who is going to act as a guardian, regardless of where they live. Similar guidelines are expressed in the laws of other parts of Canada as well.

The following is a paraphrased summary of what the Northwest Territories' act says. In deciding what decision is in the best interests of the dependent adult, the guardian shall take the following into consideration:

- If the guardian knows of a wish or instruction that was expressed by the dependent adult when the dependent adult was still mentally capable, the guardian shall make decisions in accordance with that wish or instruction.

- If the dependent adult's current wishes can be determined, then the guardian shall make decisions in accordance with the dependent adult's current wishes.

- A guardian shall encourage the dependent adult to participate, to the best of his or her ability, in the guardian's decisions.

- A guardian shall foster regular personal contact between the dependent adult and his or her supportive friends and family.

- A guardian shall consult from time to time with the dependent adult's supportive friends and family as well as the dependent adult's caregivers.

- A guardian shall foster the dependent adult's independence as much as possible.

Guardian is the term used in most Canadian provinces and territories, but some provinces call a court-appointed guardian by a different name. See Table 2 for the names used in each province and territory.

Table 2
COURT-APPOINTED GUARDIAN NAMES BY PROVINCE AND TERRITORY

Province and Territory	Court-Appointed Guardian Names
Alberta	Guardian
British Columbia	Committee of person
Manitoba	Committee for personal care
New Brunswick	Committee of person
Newfoundland and Labrador	Guardian
Northwest Territories	Guardian
Nova Scotia	Guardian
Nunavut	Guardian
Ontario	Guardian
Prince Edward Island	Guardian
Saskatchewan	Personal guardian
Yukon	Guardian

Chapters 5 and 6 will tell you more about what is involved in being a guardian.

1.2 Trusteeship

A trustee makes decisions about money, real estate, and personal property. Often there must be cooperation between the guardian and trustee if they are different people, such as the case in which a dependent adult is moved from his or her residence to live in a long-term care facility. The guardian chooses which facility is appropriate. The trustee arranges for the paying of the facility's bills. The trustee may also, depending on the situation, arrange to sell the dependent adult's home, clear out and distribute the contents of the house, and invest the sale proceeds on behalf of the dependent adult. In this way, both guardianship and trusteeship roles are called upon.

In law, a trustee is anyone who holds onto or looks after money or property for someone else. If you are the trustee, you have control of the money or property, but you do not own it. As the trustee, you are not holding the money or property for your own benefit or for the benefit of your family or friends. You are not entitled to use it for anyone but the dependent adult and his or her dependants. You are holding on to the property and money and managing them on behalf of the dependent adult. You are called a trustee because you have been entrusted to be the caretaker of someone else's property.

You should note that in legal documents, when the phrase *money or property* is used, the word *property* does not just mean real estate. This can sometimes be confusing, because when the word property is used in a non-law context, it usually means a house or land.

When talking about trusteeship, property can mean both real estate (e.g., land, house, revenue property, summer cottage, or mineral lease) and personal property (e.g., money, vehicle, mobile home, jewellery, furniture, clothing, tools, machinery, livestock, inheritance, investments, mutual funds, bonds, collections, artwork, corporate shares, intellectual property, and almost anything else that is not real estate). Throughout this book, the word property will mean both real and personal property.

It is essential to note that being appointed as a trustee does not give you permission to do whatever you want with the dependent adult's property. There is a widespread impression among Canadians that a trustee, once appointed by the court, can do whatever he or she wants with the money. Nothing could be further from the truth. As a trustee you must carefully read the court order that appoints you so that you know the limits of your authority. In addition, there are laws in place that put restrictions on what all trustees can do, even though those laws may not be mentioned on the specific court order. If you intentionally or carelessly cause a financial loss to a dependent adult, you can be held personally liable for that loss. Chapter 8 will tell you more about the restrictions placed on a trustee by law.

A trustee is a *fiduciary*. This word describes a legal relationship in which the trustee must always, without fail, act in the best interests of the dependent adult, even if doing so means he or she acts *against* his or her own interests. This is not always easy to understand or to do. By agreeing to act as trustee, the trustee is willingly taking on a role in which he or she always acts in a way that is intended to benefit the dependent adult.

Across Canada, the role of a court-appointed trustee is called by one of three names, those being trustee, committee, or guardian. Table 3 lists the names for each province and territory.

Regardless of what this role is called in your province or territory, this book will, for ease of reading, refer to someone appointed to look after another person's property as a trustee. However, the forms on the CD use the correct term for each province and territory.

Chapters 7 through 10 will tell you more about trusteeship.

2. Provinces and Territory with Special Situations

Manitoba, Nova Scotia, and Nunavut have special situations when it comes to guardianship and trusteeship. The following sections explain the special situations you may encounter if you are dealing with the law in those provinces and territory.

2.1 Manitoba

In Manitoba, there are two laws that have to do with being appointed as the guardian and/or trustee of an adult. One is the Mental

Table 3
COURT-APPOINTED TRUSTEE NAMES BY PROVINCE AND TERRITORY

Province and Territory	Name for Trustee
Alberta	Trustee
British Columbia	Committee of estate
Manitoba	Committee for property
New Brunswick	Committee of estate
Newfoundland and Labrador	Guardian
Northwest Territories	Trustee
Nova Scotia	Guardian
Nunavut	Trustee
Ontario	Guardian of property
Prince Edward Island	Committee
Saskatchewan	Property guardian
Yukon	Guardian

Health Act and the other is the Vulnerable Persons Living with a Disability Act. The procedures and forms are very different for the two laws and anyone who wants to make a court application to become someone's guardian or trustee must figure out which procedure he or she is to follow.

The Vulnerable Persons Living with a Disability Act only applies to an adult who loses his or her capacity if that incapacity manifests itself *before* the adult reaches adulthood. This would not appear to be relevant to the people we are most concerned about in this book. Given that this book focuses on elderly people who are losing their capacity due to aging, it is highly unlikely that this act will apply. Therefore, residents of Manitoba will find that this book focuses only on applications that may be made under the Mental Health Act.

In the event that you are not sure which procedure applies to your situation, you may wish to discuss it with the very helpful and approachable staff of the Office of the Vulnerable Persons' Commissioner in Winnipeg. Contact information is available on the CD.

2.2 Nova Scotia

In Nova Scotia, most applications for the appointment of guardians are made under the Incompetent Persons Act. However, Nova Scotia also has a second way of being appointed as the guardian of an adult person who has lost capacity, that being the Inebriate's Guardianship Act. The procedure is the same. As may seem obvious, the latter act specifically refers to a loss of capacity that is brought around by a person's habitual drunkenness and is not specifically related to aging. As the focus of this book is on incapacity due to aging, all of the forms and information in this

book will refer to the Incompetent Persons Act only.

2.3 Nunavut

When Nunavut became Canada's newest territory in 1999 by splitting off from the Northwest Territories, it retained some of the laws of the Northwest Territories and adopted them as their own. One of the laws of the Northwest Territories that still applies in Nunavut is the Guardianship and Trusteeship Act, which sets out the rules, procedures, and forms for the appointment of guardians and trustees for adults. Therefore, all of the information in this book that applies to the Northwest Territories also applies to Nunavut.

You will note that there are a few changes to the forms that are used for making your application. For example, you must refer to the Nunavut Court of Justice rather than the Northwest Territories court. These changes have already been made on the forms for Nunavut readers.

3. In the Best Interests of the Dependent Adult

There are not a lot of legal guidelines as to what does and does not constitute acting in the best interests of a dependent adult and it may not be easy for you to determine what is in the best interests of your elderly relative. Obviously acting in his or her best interests cannot mean that you only do what the dependent adult wants, as some of the wishes expressed by a dependent adult may be unreasonable. After all, you would not be in the position of guardian and trustee in the first place if the dependent adult was fully capable of making all his or her own decisions.

For example, many elderly people are understandably distraught at the thought of leaving their homes and moving into long-term care facilities or at the need to give up driving their own vehicles. This is often seen by the dependent adult as more of a punishment than anything as it represents a severe loss of freedom, independence, and even identity. However, you, as the guardian, may have no choice but to take steps to move the dependent adult or to have his or her driver's licence revoked if the dependent adult simply cannot manage safely on his or her own any longer. In a case like that, what the dependent adult wants and what is in his or her best interest are not the same.

The wishes and intentions of a dependent adult should always be taken into consideration whenever it is possible to do so. Not all dependent adults suffer from a problem so severe that they can have no input whatsoever into things such as selection of birthday gifts for grandchildren, plans for vacation, or whether they need to see a doctor. Where the dependent adult is able to offer input that is reasonable in the circumstances, it is in the best interest of the dependent adult for that input to be heard and acted upon. Remember that you, as a guardian and trustee, have agreed to act in the least restrictive manner possible and you should remain open to opinions expressed by the dependent adult.

A mistake that is frequently made by children who become guardians of their parents is to set up matters in a way that is convenient for themselves, regardless of whether it is enjoyable, comfortable, or agreeable for the parents. This can lead to neglect and even abuse.

It is absolutely essential that you work with your elderly relative to try to determine his or her wishes and to work within them whenever possible.

In determining whether having a guardian or trustee appointed for your elderly relative is in the elderly relative's best interests, consider the following questions:

- Can the elderly relative make all personal and financial decisions for himself or herself safely and happily right now?

- If so, how long is that situation likely to continue?

- How would the elderly relative's life be improved in the short term and in the long term by having a guardian or trustee appointed?

- What risk is the elderly relative running by refusing decision-making help?

- Is there an urgent situation existing right now that must be addressed quickly?

- Are there any solutions available that are less intrusive than a court-appointed guardianship or trusteeship? (See Chapter 3 regarding alternatives.)

- Has the elderly relative ever made any suggestions or given any instructions about who he or she would like to live with or who he or she would like to have in charge of his or her affairs?

Chapter 2 may help you answer these questions.

2

DOES YOUR PARENT NEED A GUARDIAN OR TRUSTEE?

Loss of mental capacity in an adult will be diagnosed and documented by a doctor or psychologist if an application is going to be made to the court. However, in most cases, a dependent adult's family members are the ones who first notice there is a problem such as memory loss or an inability to do things the elderly relative used to do. The family members are the ones who have the opportunity to observe their elderly relative on a regular basis and to notice when the relative is having problems living independently. The family members usually then take the relative to a doctor for a diagnosis.

It can be difficult to know when it is time to become involved as a guardian or trustee. The following two sections describe some common behavioural symptoms shown by elderly relatives who are experiencing some loss of capacity. The lists in the following sections

are not intended to be medical advice that can replace a consultation with a doctor. They are merely lists of symptoms or problems that are frequently documented by medical reports that are used in guardianship and trusteeship applications. Please note that every individual is unique and may exhibit some, none, or all of these behaviours.

Please also keep in mind that there could be medical explanations other than lack of capacity for isolated symptoms and you should rely on a doctor for help with interpreting your relative's specific situation. For example, sometimes a person giving inappropriate answers to questions is confused and forgetful and this might be a symptom of incapacity. However, it is also possible that the person may not be mentally incapable at all but is giving inappropriate answers simply because he or she is hard of hearing. If you believe that your elderly relative is exhibiting some of these behaviours and that they may point to a loss of capacity, the first step should be to ensure that your relative is under the care of a physician who can rule out other diagnoses.

1. Indications That Guardianship Might be Necessary

Your elderly parent might need a guardian to assist with *personal- and health-care decisions* if he or she —

- is unable to safely prepare meals for himself or herself, leaves pots and pans on the stove to boil dry, repeatedly scalds himself or herself with hot water, starts kitchen fires, or has problems remembering how to carry out other daily tasks that used to be familiar;

- becomes disoriented when he or she leaves home, forgets his or her address, or forgets how to get home;

- fails to recognize people he or she has known for a long time;

- is unable to maintain personal hygiene on his or her own (e.g., bathing, toileting, dental care, grooming) or is unaware that hygiene is a problem;

- is unable to manage a condition or illness on his or her own, forgets to take essential medication or treatment, or because of memory loss, takes too much medicine;

- is unable to safely transfer from a wheelchair to bed, toilet, etc., on his or her own;

- neglects medical or dental appointments, does not know how to make appointments, or is unable to get to appointments on his or her own;

- forgets to shop for food, toiletries, and other essentials or is physically unable to shop for essentials on his or her own;

- is unable to maintain his or her home in a safe, hygienic manner, neglects to repair broken windows or appliances, hoards items (e.g., newspapers) to the point that they become a hazard, fails to take out garbage regularly, or neglects to clean up after pets;

- often puts things in the wrong places, for example, putting the telephone in the refrigerator;

- is experiencing more and more memory loss;

- has undergone a noticeable personality change or has become unpredictable; and/or

- would not be able to get out of the house quickly on his or her own in the event of fire.

2. Indications That Trusteeship Might be Necessary

Your elderly parent might need a trustee to assist with *financial decision making* if he or she —

- has been taken advantage of financially by scam artists, strangers, or family members;

- answers the door to strangers and is susceptible to being taken advantage of by them financially;

- is making irrational changes to his or her will;

- is transferring assets to friends or family members for no apparent reason, such as selling property to them for less than market value or placing bank accounts in joint names;

- forgets to pay bills, resulting in essential services such as telephone, heat, or water being disconnected;

- forgets that he or she has already paid bills and pays them repeatedly;

- misplaces money, pension cheques, bills, or important paperwork;

- cannot manage small financial transactions such as store purchases or restaurant meals that he or she used to be able to manage;

- neglects to deposit cheques in the bank;

- neglects to complete tax returns;

- unwittingly lives beyond his or her means due to extravagant gifts, charitable donations, or purchases that appear to indicate that he or she does not understand the value of money or the economics of his or her household;

- makes irrational, unnecessary purchases, such as buying cans of dog food when he or she does not own a dog;

- makes large cash withdrawals for which there is no corresponding purchase or bill payment and cannot recall where he or she spent the money;

- has made a recent friend — usually of the opposite sex — who seems to exert a lot of influence on him or her and to whom he or she is giving money or property; and/or

- is physically unable to get to the bank on his or her own.

3. Identifying Mental Incapacity

The behaviours mentioned in sections 1 and 2 can be seen in many elderly people who are beginning to lose their mental competence. However, unless you are a doctor, it is not easy to understand what these behaviours mean or why they are occurring. Loss of mental capacity may be due to any one of a dozen causes. In many cases, loss of capacity is progressive in elderly people, meaning that the possibility of recovering capacity is slim. Only a doctor can tell you for sure whether this is happening to your elderly relative.

Loss of mental capacity is rarely all or nothing, especially in the early stages. Keep in mind that your elderly relative may be perfectly capable of independence in some areas while losing his or her ability to deal with another area. This is why guardianship and trusteeship are in most parts of Canada considered to be two different jobs; not every dependent adult needs help with all areas of living.

You should consult with a doctor to try to understand how your elderly relative's condition will affect him or her now and in the future. By consulting with your elderly relative's doctor, you may be able to predict the kind of care your relative will need in the future. You can then work within the legal system to set up the protection and assistance that is needed. The level and type of assistance needed may well change over time.

As a cautionary note, try not to jump to conclusions about an elderly relative's capacity regarding money. It is important to understand that an elderly relative may make financial decisions that you do not like. This does not necessarily mean that the relative has lost mental capacity. Generally speaking, an adult does not require the approval of other adults (even if those adults are his or her children) when spending his or her own money. Most of us can think of friends who choose to use their money for gambling, risky investments, expensive leisure equipment, or the support of a particular individual. Often these are choices with which we may not agree but we do not interfere, recognizing that individual's right to spend his or her own money as he or she sees fit.

As an adult, your elderly relative has the same right as anyone else to decide what he or she wants to do with his or her money, even if the person's choices may look odd or foolish to other people. It is only when it becomes apparent that the odd decisions are being made because your elderly relative is suffering from memory loss, disorientation, or influence by an unscrupulous person that mental capacity becomes an issue. Make sure that you are not imposing your own wishes or values on your elderly relative; your goal is to make sure that he or she is still able to express his or her own wishes.

4. Medical Evidence You Will Need

If you make an application to the court to become a guardian or trustee, you will need medical paperwork to support your application. Specifically, the medical paperwork must prove your claim that the dependent adult suffers from a loss of mental capacity. A court is simply not going to take away an individual's right to manage his or her own affairs unless the court is given proof that the person cannot manage on his or her own any longer. This proof is always given by people other than the person applying to be the guardian or trustee (i.e., independent third parties who have nothing to gain or lose from you being appointed as guardian or trustee).

The medical reports or affidavits that you obtain as part of your court application will serve two purposes. The first is to protect your elderly relative from unscrupulous people who try to gain control over the relative's finances for fraudulent purposes by making it appear that the elderly person cannot make his or her own decisions. The requirement that the evidence be independent makes fraud more difficult. Fraud does not only happen to wealthy seniors; it can and does happen to those with modest assets as well, and all elderly persons are entitled to the protection of the law.

The second purpose is to assist a judge who will usually not even meet or see the dependent adult during the course of your application. The judge needs to be able to decide what is in the best interests of the elderly relative and relies on the reports to provide the needed information. Because all of the laws pertaining to dependent adults make it very clear that a loss of ability to make one's own decisions is a prerequisite to anyone being appointed as a guardian and trustee, it is up to the person making the court application to prove to the judge that a guardianship or trusteeship is actually needed.

Make sure that the medical forms are properly completed, signed, and dated, and that you are not relying on outdated information — medical information more than six months old may be considered unreliable. Make sure that all of your paperwork for the court is carefully and thoroughly prepared so that the court can make an informed decision.

The list below gives details about the various forms needed in each province and territory and who should be completing the forms. All of the forms can be found on the CD that accompanies this book. Make sure that you are giving the court *original* documents and not photocopies or fax copies.

Alberta

You will need a Form 1: Report of Physician or Psychologist (DAD16) to be signed by a medical doctor or a psychologist. You will also need a Functional Assessment Report (DAD17), which is usually completed by a hands-on caregiver such as a nurse, therapist, or social worker.

British Columbia

You will need two Affidavits by Doctor, completed by two medical doctors. As there is no specific form requested by the legislation, you will follow the general form for affidavits under the Rules of Court. The wording given in the forms that accompany this book is suggested wording only and is not mandated by the Rules of Court. You may change the wording to suit your own specific set of circumstances.

Manitoba

You will need two Affidavits of Doctor, completed by at least two medical doctors. As there is no specific form requested by the legislation, you will follow the general form for affidavits under the Rules of Court. The wording given in the forms that accompany this book is suggested wording only and is not mandated by the Rules of Court. You may change the wording to suit your own specific set of circumstances.

New Brunswick

You will need at least one Affidavit of Doctor from a medical practitioner and at least one Affidavit of Person Acquainted with the Respondent from a person acquainted with the dependent adult. As there is no specific form requested by the legislation, you will follow the general form for affidavits under the Rules of Court. The wording given in the forms that accompany this book is suggested wording only and is not mandated by the Rules of Court. You may change the wording to suit your own specific set of circumstances.

Newfoundland and Labrador

You will need an affidavit, though the law does not state from whom you should get the affidavit. As every other jurisdiction specifically states that this evidence must be given by a medical doctor it would seem logical that a medical doctor would be the best choice in this case as well. As there is no specific form requested by the legislation, you will follow the general form for affidavits under the Rules of Court. The wording given in the forms that accompany this book is suggested wording only and is not mandated by the Rules of Court. You may change the wording to suit your own specific set of circumstances.

Northwest Territories and Nunavut

You will need a medical report in Form 1: Assessment Report. The form must be completed by a medical doctor, a psychologist, or a person who is assigned the responsibility of preparing the report by the Office of the Public Guardian.

Nova Scotia

You will need affidavits from two medical doctors. As there is no specific form requested by the legislation, you will follow the general form for affidavits under the Rules of Court. The wording given in the forms that accompany this book is suggested wording only and is not mandated by the Rules of Court. You may change the wording to suit your own specific set of circumstances.

Ontario

You will need two assessments. The assessments must be completed by a medical doctor, psychologist, social worker, occupational therapist, or registered nurse. The form needed will depend on the application being made. Form A is needed for the appointment of a guardian for property (equivalent to a trustee) and Form B is needed for the appointment of a guardian of the person.

Prince Edward Island

You will need two assessments in Form 13: Certificate of Incapacity to Manage Personal Affairs, both of which must be signed by medical doctors.

Saskatchewan

You will need two medical reports, both in Form J. You can use more than two reports if that is appropriate. The forms may be completed by a medical doctor, psychologist, psychiatric nurse, registered nurse, occupational therapist, or speech-language pathologist.

Yukon

You will need one Incapability Assessment Report (Form 6), which must be completed by a medical doctor, registered nurse, psychologist, or occupational therapist.

4.1   The best medical evidence

When obtaining any doctor's, nurse's, or psychologist's report it is best to try to get the report from a professional who has known the dependent adult for some time or who is currently treating the dependent adult. This is because you want to get the most accurate report possible — one that will neither exaggerate the dependent adult's problems nor minimize them. A lot of people will be relying on these reports for many years and accuracy is essential. An elderly relative that is taken, perhaps unwillingly, to a stranger for examination will feel stress, apprehension, and possibly even disorientation. He or she will therefore not be functioning at his or her best and the doctor may get a false picture of the patient's condition. This simply is not fair to the dependent adult and you should make every effort to involve a doctor with whom the dependent adult is already familiar.

In addition, in a short visit a doctor may make an assessment based on an unfamiliar patient's performance without being made aware that the patient normally uses a hearing aid, wears glasses, or relies on a language interpreter. Again, in this situation the doctor may be presented with a less than accurate picture of the patient's ability to function and as a result the report issued by the doctor will be flawed.

In many larger centres in Canada, there are doctors available who specialize in geriatrics (i.e., health care for older people). Large cities generally have entire hospitals or hospital departments devoted to the care of older people. You should consider this kind of doctor if one is available to you. To find out whether there is a geriatric specialist in or near your town, you could ask your family doctor, call a major hospital nearby, or contact a local group concerned with elder issues, such as groups that assist families to deal with Alzheimer's disease or a seniors' advocacy group.

4.2 How to get the medical evidence

In parts of Canada in which there is a specific form required by law, you should print the form and take it with you to the dependent adult's doctor, preferably on the visit at which he or she is examining the dependent adult. Explain that you wish to apply to the court to be appointed as guardian or trustee and give the doctor the form. Ask him or her to complete, sign, and date the form (all medical forms *must* be signed and dated by the doctor). You may not receive the form back immediately, as the doctor may wish to run some tests, see the dependent adult a second time, review the dependent adult's medical history,

or consult with another doctor. Once the medical form is returned to you, it will become part of your signed and sworn application to the court.

In the areas of Canada in which there is no specific form and the medical evidence must be supplied by way of affidavit, the process is slightly more complicated. All evidence given to the judge must be sworn to be true, either by you or by the doctor. One of two things can happen. The first is that the doctor will see the dependent adult and provide you with a written report. You will then prepare an affidavit for the doctor to sign, in which the doctor will swear that he or she prepared the report and believes it to be accurate. The report will be Exhibit "A" to the affidavit. This affidavit will form part of the court application. Because the affidavit is evidence, the doctor will have to swear it in front of a Commissioner for Oaths, so again, you may have to come back at a later date once the doctor has had a chance to do that.

The second possibility is that the doctor will provide you not with a separate report but with an affidavit already sworn before a Commissioner for Oaths. You are more likely to have this happen if you prepare the affidavit ahead of time and take it with you when you take the dependent adult to the doctor. You can then leave the affidavit with the doctor, thereby eliminating one step from the procedure.

3

ALTERNATIVES TO APPLYING FOR
COURT-ORDERED GUARDIANSHIP
AND TRUSTEESHIP

1. Why You Should Consider Alternatives

Before deciding to make an application to the court to be appointed as guardian and/or trustee, it is worthwhile to take the time to consider whether there are any alternatives available. Each elderly person's situation and needs are unique, and it may be the case that those needs can be met by measures that are less expensive and less intrusive than having a guardian and trustee appointed. For example, a senior living alone might have no trouble doing his or her banking and looking after investment transactions but might have physical limitations. It might be possible to avoid the expense and trouble of having a guardian appointed for this person if someone could accompany him or her to the bank on a regular basis. Being appointed as a guardian and trustee should be a last resort.

Alternatives should be explored for two reasons. The first reason is that guardianship and trusteeship can be invasive to an individual dependent adult. The second reason is that court applications can be expensive and may deplete a modest estate unnecessarily.

In many jurisdictions in Canada, the law expressly says that no guardian or trustee can be appointed if there are alternatives available. In Saskatchewan, for example, if you are applying to be a guardian or trustee of a dependent adult, you will be required to first show the court that other, less intrusive methods of assisting the dependent adult have been tried or at least seriously considered. In the Northwest Territories, the court will not

16

make a trusteeship order unless it is satisfied that there is no alternative available that is less restrictive of the decision-making rights of the dependent adult. Other provinces have similar wording. Not all jurisdictions have this kind of requirement stated right in the law itself, but the concept of using the courts as a last resort is well entrenched.

A number of alternatives are described in this chapter. Some of them address guardianship issues and some address trusteeship issues. Not every alternative will suit every person. If one of the alternatives (or a combination of them) seems like a solution for a particular elderly relative about whom you are concerned, it is worthwhile to explore that alternative with family members, doctors, and caregivers who care about your relative.

2. Informal Trusteeship

If your elderly relative is receiving benefits from the federal Government, including Old Age Security, Canada Pension Plan, Guaranteed Income Supplement, Spouse's Allowance, or Survivor's Allowance, it may be possible for a family member to apply directly to the government to become an informal trustee. This is different from a court-ordered trusteeship in many ways, the main difference being that the informal trustee only has authority to deal with the government benefits. This means, for example, that an informal trustee would have the power to deposit the Old Age Security or Canada Pension Plan cheques and use the money to pay bills, but would not have the power to deal with any other property owned by the dependent adult, such as the dependent adult's house, investments, or money inherited under an estate. In other words, this kind of informal trusteeship is really only

meant for people who do not have other assets besides the government benefits.

However, if the only asset needing attention at the moment is a government pension or benefit, then this option is definitely worth considering. No court application is involved in this process, which means that there are no court fees, no service of documents on other people, and fewer delays. Application for informal trusteeship is made through the Government of Canada, Income Security Programs. They have offices in all provinces and territories as well as a toll-free number (1-800-277-9914).

In order to make an application for informal trusteeship, two forms must be filled out and provided to the government. The first is the Certificate of Incapability, a form that must be completed and signed by the dependent adult's doctor to provide evidence that the person really does require assistance. The second is the Undertaking to Administer Benefits Under the Old Age Security Act and/or the Canada Pension Plan Act. These forms, as well as assistance in completing them, can be obtained by calling the toll-free number mentioned above. By calling this number, you can also, if you wish, discuss whether informal trusteeship is the right choice for you and your elderly relative.

You can also complete the forms online by accessing the Government of Canada website. These forms are in PDF format so that you complete them by typing the information in the fields provided, and then print the completed forms and mail them to the address provided on the website.

A similar informal trusteeship is also available through Veterans Affairs Canada for seniors who are receiving benefits from that department. In addition, provincial aid programs for individuals with mental or physical disabilities that prevent them from working also allow and encourage informal trusteeship. If your elderly relative is receiving disability benefits of any kind from the government, you can inquire about informal trusteeship to the program that pays the benefits.

If you become an informal trustee for your relative, you will have the legal authority to collect the dependent adult's monthly cheque, deposit the cheque in the bank, and use the money to pay the dependent adult's bills. It does not give you the authority to use any of the dependent adult's money for yourself or to pay yourself. Nor does it give you the authority to touch any of the dependent adult's other money or property.

One of the advantages of informal trusteeship is the initial cost of becoming a trustee, which is significantly less because no application to the court is required. Another advantage is the simplicity and quickness of the application process. There is also the advantage that informal trustees are not required to make appearances in front of a judge to account for their trusteeship.

The disadvantage is that the scope of the informal trustee's authority is limited only to the government benefit and not any other assets of the dependent adult. You should consider both the advantages and the disadvantages when determining whether this approach would work for you.

3. In-Home Support

If the issues facing your relative are largely due to physical limitations and not loss of mental capacity, you might consider assisting your relative to continue to live in his or her own home, if he or she so wishes. This may be possible if you can make arrangements for appropriate in-home support.

The move to a senior's residence or long-term care facility can in itself trigger the need for a guardianship order because it removes an elderly person from familiar surroundings and an existing support system. Helping your relative live at home longer could prevent, or at least postpone, the need to apply to the court for a guardianship order.

The test for whether or not an elderly relative can and should be assisted with living in his or her own home with support is, of course, whether staying at home is in the best interests of that elderly relative. Continuing to live in his or her own home could be in the best interests of an elderly person who does not wish to move away from an area that includes his or her friends, place of worship, children, or convenient services. Removing a person in this situation from his or her home would in effect deprive this person of friends, social network, or ability to attend church. This tends to add to loneliness, isolation, and unhappiness for older people.

Many older individuals also have a strong sentimental attachment to the home in which they lived their married lives and raised their children and do not want to leave their homes until it becomes absolutely necessary to do so. The emotional impact of leaving the home should be taken into consideration if at all possible.

Prospective guardians should respect the dependent adult's wish to remain at home as long as it is feasible to do so. This wish to remain in the home must be balanced against practical concerns such as safety, mobility, nutrition, and hygiene.

In most large- and mid-sized communities in Canada, you will be able to arrange for nurses or nursing aides to come into the dependent adult's home on a regular basis. Nurses can assist your elderly relative with taking medication or giving injections, or with specialized medical needs such as foot care for diabetics or physical therapy. Aides may provide help with bathing, personal grooming, and transfer from bed to wheelchair. In small communities you may not have access to trained personnel and private service companies as easily as you would in a large city. However, you may find there is more support from family, friends, and neighbours who live nearby and who are willing to take on some of these tasks.

Other valuable in-home resources are companies, organizations, or individuals that will —

- bring nutritious, prepared meals to the dependent adult's home;

- do housecleaning on a regular or occasional basis;

- transport senior citizens to appointments;

- shovel snow and clear walkways;

- rake leaves and mow grass;

- walk the dependent adult's dog;

- do small repairs and handyman jobs;

- deliver groceries; and

- deliver prescriptions.

Another factor that will likely be part of your evaluation of whether remaining in the home is in the best interest of your elderly relative is the cost of these services. Seniors may find that living on a fixed income does not allow for the payment for these services. If you are exploring this option, be sure to contact federal and provincial government agencies to ensure that you are aware of all funding and benefits that are available.

Another good idea is to make sure that your elderly relative has a cellular telephone and that he or she has it when away from home. It can be invaluable in emergency situations. If remembering telephone numbers is a problem, program them into the telephone's memory and show your relative how to access the telephone directory or speed-dial feature on the phone.

If you are looking into support services that will allow your relative to stay in his or her home, you might also consider whether renovations need to be made to the home for the safety and convenience of your relative. For example, you may need to have a wheelchair ramp built, grab-bars installed in the bathroom, or area rugs replaced by carpeting. Some provinces have government subsidies for this kind of renovation. Many of the suggestions in this section will also apply if you are considering moving your elderly relative into your own family home.

4. Placing Assets in Joint Names

Although this particular alternative is fraught with potential problems, it can be a good solution for a limited number of families. Using this alternative should be approached with a great deal of caution. Think it through carefully.

The basic idea is to put an asset that is currently owned only by the elderly relative, usually a bank account, into joint names. The dependent adult would be one of the joint owners and another person, usually a child of the dependent adult, would be the other owner. The purpose of doing this is to allow the child access to the bank account so that the dependent adult's pension and other cheques can be deposited and monthly bills can be paid. The advantages of taking this approach are that it is quick to set up, simple to operate, and there is no court involvement.

Sometimes, however, this arrangement is much more to the advantage of the child than the dependent adult. There is a huge risk that the dependent adult's money could disappear and this risk should be very carefully considered. Many an otherwise honest person has dipped into his or her parent's funds to cover short-term losses, only to find he or she could not replace the money. In other cases, if the child owes money to a third party, the joint bank account could be garnished to satisfy a debt, causing the parent to lose his or her savings. There is little or no protection for the dependent adult in any of these situations if he or she has voluntarily set up a joint bank account with the child.

The other major problem with jointly held assets is the distribution of those assets when the dependent adult dies. Any asset that is jointly owned, such as a joint bank account, gives both owners a right of survivorship. This means if the dependent adult and his or her child jointly own a bank account, when one of them dies the other one automatically owns the whole bank account. This can have serious ramifications within a family and can be the cause of bitter disputes, particularly if it interferes with an estate plan contemplated by the

dependent adult. Consider all aspects of this approach, including how it looks to other family members, before going ahead.

For example, if Mr. Smith owns $15,000, he might put $5,000 into a GIC in his own name and the remaining $10,000 into a joint bank account with his son, Jim. Even though Mr. Smith's intention was only to give Jim access so that he could help with the banking, when Mr. Smith dies, Jim will own the $10,000 in the account. If Mr. Smith has three other children who will share the $5,000 GIC between them, they might be quite upset at the fact that Jim has received so much more money than they have. Perhaps Mr. Smith trusted Jim to divide the money among his siblings. Or, maybe he wanted Jim to own the money. You will have only Jim's word for it. This could lead to a bitter, expensive dispute if the siblings believe that Jim influenced, or attempted to influence, their father for monetary gain.

It is never a good idea to ask an elderly relative to put his or her home (or other real estate) into joint names with yourself or any other person without ensuring that the elderly relative sees a lawyer on his or her own to discuss the transaction first. You should not attend that meeting with the lawyer. Let your elderly relative handle the matter on his or her own. If the elderly relative does not understand the transaction or its effects well enough to explain them to a lawyer on his or her own then clearly your elderly relative does not understand what it means to sign over title to the home. Legal documents should not be signed by individuals who do not understand what the documents are and the effect they will have.

A useful legal document sometimes used in conjunction with putting assets in joint names is a bare trust. This brief document simply states that although the asset is in joint names, the elderly relative does not intend that his or her child will own the property after the parent's death. The document specifically states that the child's name was only put on the asset for convenience. It is not a good idea to try to draft a trust like this on your own; it is better to have that done by a lawyer. It can be done quickly and inexpensively by a lawyer.

5. Health Care Directive

This document goes by various names across Canada, such as Health Care Directive, Advance Health Care Directive, Advance Directive, Personal Directive, and Power of Attorney for Personal Care. It will be referred to as a Health Care Directive in this book. Though it goes by various names, it has one main purpose: it names an individual to act as a spokesperson and decision maker for an elderly person who is unable to make or communicate his or her own decisions about personal and health matters.

The type of decisions that can be made by a person (called an agent in this book) appointed under a Health Care Directive roughly corresponds with the type of decisions that would be made by a court-appointed guardian. This would include medical decisions about surgery, tests, treatments, and medications. It would also include other personal decisions such as where and how the elderly relative will live. If a valid Health Care Directive is in place, it is highly unlikely that anyone will need to be appointed by the court as guardian.

This is not a document that you can impose on your elderly relative by applying to the court for an order. The courts are not involved at all in creating the Health Care Directive. The Health Care Directive is signed by the elderly relative and it is an expression of his or her wishes. By signing this kind of document, the elderly relative has the opportunity to choose a spokesperson for himself or herself as opposed to having the choice imposed on him or her by other people. The elderly person also gets to express his or her thoughts about whether or not he or she wishes to donate organs after death or be kept alive artificially, if in a vegetative state.

Estate planning lawyers encourage their clients to sign this very useful document well in advance of any mental or physical problems arising. That way, the document is ready to be used when it is needed and the family need not go to the expense, delay, stress, and possible disputes of applying to the court to appoint a guardian. However, not everyone has signed a Health Care Directive, either because they had no opportunity to do so or because they chose not to do so. It is important to note that if your elderly relative has already lost his or her mental ability to understand legal documents, it may be too late for him or her to sign a Health Care Directive.

If you are not sure whether your relative has capacity, you should discuss this with his or her regular doctor. Capacity is a complex concept. A person who has lost capacity to do one thing, such as deal with money, may not necessarily have lost capacity with respect to other things.

If your elderly relative still does have the mental capacity to understand the nature of a Health Care Directive and understand what it would mean to sign one, this might be a viable alternative to involving the courts. It is beyond the scope of this book to give instructions on how the document is to be prepared. You may assist your elderly relative in seeing a lawyer to have this document prepared, or you may look for a self-help book that gives instructions on how to prepare a Health Care Directive. For more information see the *Power of Attorney Kit*, another book published by Self-Counsel Press.

In the event that your elderly relative does already have a Health Care Directive in place, you should read the document carefully to determine whether it can be used in your situation instead of applying to the court for a guardian. The document will tell you, first of all, who the relative has chosen as his or her spokesperson. It might not be a person you would have chosen but you will have to live with that choice. The document can only be used by the person named in it. It will also give some guidance as to the health care preferred by the relative. If you doubt the document's validity, you might consult an estate-planning lawyer to review the Health Care Directive. Assuming that the document is valid, it can be presented to the hospital or other facility in which the relative is to be treated or admitted, without any court involvement whatsoever.

6. Representation Agreements

In British Columbia, Saskatchewan, and the Yukon, it is possible to make written agreements known as Representation Agreements between a dependent adult and one or more trusted friends or relatives who are willing to assist the dependent adult with decision making.

Representation Agreements are different from Health Care Directives in one very important way. A Health Care Directive simply appoints a decision maker who is not the dependent adult. The Representation Agreement appoints someone to make decisions *with* the dependent adult, not *for* the dependent adult. In both kinds of documents, the person who helps with decisions is appointed by the dependent adult, but with the Representation Agreement the dependent adult can choose to keep some decision-making ability for himself or herself.

It is not the purpose of this book to give specific instructions on how these agreements are to be made. If, after reading these sections, you believe that this alternative would be helpful to you and your elderly relative, you can either see a lawyer to have the documents prepared or you may seek out a self-help book that specifically addresses the preparation of Representation Agreements.

6.1 Agreements in British Columbia

Representation Agreements in British Columbia are versatile documents that can either authorize a person to help the dependent adult make decisions or authorize a person (known as the *representative*) to make decisions on his or her own on behalf of the dependent adult. This is the choice of the dependent adult at the time he or she signs the document. The dependent adult has to expressly state in the document what he or she wants the role of the representative to be.

The dependent adult maintains a great deal of control over the document. He or she may give the representative power to make personal- and health-care decisions normally associated with guardianship or to make financial decisions normally associated with trusteeship or both. The dependent adult will identify the areas in which he or she needs assistance. This person can give different people the authority to make different decisions.

The dependent adult may appoint the following as his or her representative:

- The Public Guardian and Trustee.

- A credit union or trust company. This can only be done as long as the decisions made by the credit union or trust company are strictly financial decisions and not personal- or health-related decisions.

- An individual person. If the dependent person appoints an individual, the dependent adult must also appoint a monitor unless the individual appointed was a spouse, or at least two individuals are appointed who must act jointly. The monitor's job is to ensure that the representative is acting honestly, diligently, and prudently, and is consulting with the dependent adult where possible and is not acting outside his or her authority.

As with the other alternatives to court-appointed guardianship and trusteeship that are discussed in this chapter, the Representation Agreement allows a dependent adult to maintain some control over his or her own affairs. Having an agreement in place is much less intrusive than a court order. The Representation Act of British Columbia specifically says that the law was put into place to avoid the need for court applications to appoint guardians and trustees.

6.2   Co-Decision-Making in Saskatchewan

In Saskatchewan, an elderly person can sign an agreement with another person whereby the person will help the elderly person make decisions. The person selected to give that help is called a co-decision-maker. This is because he or she will help the elderly relative make his or her own decisions as much as possible, rather than stepping in to make all decisions.

The person selected can be a personal co-decision-maker who can assist with health and personal decisions. The person's job is roughly equivalent to that of a guardian. He or she may also be a property co-decision-maker who can assist with decisions respecting finances and property. This job is roughly equivalent to that of a trustee.

As with the British Columbia Representation Agreements discussed above, the Saskatchewan co-decision-making agreements are specifically allowed by law to avoid the need for guardians and trustees to be appointed by the courts. The agreements allow the elderly relative to maintain some control over decisions that affect him or her.

6.3   Agreements in the Yukon

In the Yukon, there are two kinds of agreements available. One is the Supported Decision-Making Agreement (under Part 1 of the Act) and the other is a Representation Agreement (under Part 2 of the Act). They will be discussed in more detail in the paragraphs below. It is important to know that the Yukon law specifically says that the court should not be asked to appoint full guardians or trustees unless alternatives such as these agreements have been tried or at least carefully considered. Therefore, if you intend to ask the court to appoint you as a guardian or trustee in the Yukon, you are going to have to explain why one of the two types of agreements could not have been used instead.

6.3a Supported Decision-Making Agreement (Yukon)

This arrangement is appropriate where the dependent adult who signs an agreement is not in need of a full guardianship or trusteeship because he or she retains some ability to deal with his or her own affairs, but some help is needed. The person who assists the dependent adult under a Supported Representation Agreement is called an *associate decision-maker*. You can see from the title given to this person that the agreement is intended to foster co-operative, joint decisions, as opposed to having a guardian or trustee alone make the decisions he or she thinks are appropriate. The associate decision-maker's duties are to assist the dependent adult in making decisions, expressing decisions, obtaining information, and discussing possible outcomes with the dependent adult.

The associate decision-maker may have the authority to deal with personal and health-care decisions normally associated with guardianship or financial decisions normally associated with trusteeship, or both.

This arrangement is much less intrusive to the dependent adult than a full guardianship or trusteeship. Signing a Supported Decision-Making Agreement would ensure that the dependent adult would retain the ability to make decisions and obtain information, but the assisting person would obtain the legal status to assist the dependent adult.

6.3b Representation Agreement (Yukon)

This kind of agreement is different than the Supported Decision-Making Agreement in that this kind of agreement appoints two or more people to make decisions on behalf of the dependent adult. The people who act under this kind of agreement are called *representatives*. Although the dependent adult is the one who appoints trusted friends or relatives as his or her representatives, the dependent adult is no longer the one making the decisions once the document is signed.

This kind of document can cover either the personal- and health-care decisions normally associated with guardianship or the financial decisions normally associated with trusteeship, or both. The document can and should be tailored to meet the needs of the dependent adult who is signing it. In this way, a dependent adult who only needs help with a certain kind of transaction, such as banking or investing, is not going to have unwanted help imposed on him or her for things he or she is perfectly capable of doing himself or herself, such as deciding where he or she is going to live.

7. Enduring Power of Attorney

Like the Health Care Directive, an Enduring Power of Attorney is a document that is signed by the elderly relative, usually long before it is actually needed. Note that an *Enduring* Power of Attorney is different from a regular Power of Attorney that is often used for business and banking. An Enduring Power of Attorney is specifically designed so that it can be used even though the person who signed it has lost his or her mental capacity. In Ontario, it is referred to as a Continuing Power of Attorney for Property and the word *continuing* has the same meaning as the word *enduring*.

The Enduring Power of Attorney names a person to be the elderly relative's spokesperson (referred to as his or her *attorney*). It also gives the attorney the authority to deal with the relative's real property and personal property. Most of these documents give a blanket authority so that the attorney can do anything that the relative can legally do with his or her property, subject to certain restrictions. Because the document was signed by the relative at a time when he or she had mental capacity, the document reflects the elderly person's wishes about how he or she wants his or her property dealt with while alive.

The kind of decision that may be made by an attorney under an Enduring Power of Attorney roughly corresponds with decisions that can be made by a court-appointed trustee. In other words, the attorney can make decisions about money, sale or rental of real estate, or payment of bills, but he or she has no authority to make any decisions about health or medical care.

Again, as with the Health Care Directive, if the document is not already in place and your elderly relative has lost his or her ability to understand legal documents, it is too late to have an Enduring Power of Attorney signed.

8. Temporary Guardianship and Trusteeship

The laws in some parts of Canada specifically say that a person can be appointed by the court as a guardian or trustee of another adult on a temporary basis. In other words, the court order is only intended to be in effect while some specific situation is dealt with, after which the dependent adult resumes control of his or her own affairs.

Generally speaking, a temporary guardianship or trusteeship is not particularly helpful when the person who needs a guardian or trustee is an aging relative. The incapacity that accompanies aging is rarely temporary in nature. If a temporary order were to be obtained, it is quite likely that you would find yourself renewing that temporary order or applying later on to the court for a permanent order. Therefore, this book will not go into detail about the procedures to be followed to apply for a temporary order.

9. An Important Note about Wills

Confusion often arises when well-intentioned individuals who want to look after elderly relatives find out that they are named as executor in the relative's will. These individuals then believe that they have a legal right to deal with the relative's assets while the relative is still alive. This is not the case. A will gives no power to anyone until the person who signed the will is deceased.

4

PUBLIC GUARDIAN AND PUBLIC TRUSTEE

The Office of the Public Guardian and Trustee is structured somewhat differently in various parts of Canada. For example, in some parts of the country the offices of the Public Trustee are separate from those of the Public Guardian, with separate buildings, staff, and jurisdiction. In other areas, the functions of these two offices are combined. Regardless of the structure, the Public Guardian and Trustee is always a part of the provincial or territorial government, either part of the Department of Justice or the Department of the Attorney General. In all provinces and territories, you can find out more about the Public Guardian and Public Trustee online by accessing the government website.

This chapter will focus on people interested in having a guardian and/or a trustee appointed for an adult. Despite the structural differences already mentioned, there are some areas in which the Office of the Public Guardian and Trustee are quite similar everywhere in Canada.

1. The Public Guardian and Trustee as Guardian/Trustee for Your Elderly Relative

One of the functions of the Office of the Public Guardian and Trustee is to act as a guardian and trustee for adults who have lost capacity. However, this function is very poorly understood in general. A common misconception is that the Office of the Public Guardian and Trustee *must* fulfill this role for everyone who needs a guardian or trustee. This is not the case. A similar misconception is that the Office of the Public Guardian and Trustee is available as an option for anyone who chooses to appoint it. That is also false.

The Public Guardian and Public Trustee should be appointed only as a last resort. In many parts of Canada, its status as last resort is specifically written into the law itself. It should not be appointed as a guardian or trustee for an individual who has family members or friends who are capable of acting as guardians and trustees and who are willing and suitable to act.

In some parts of Canada, once a certificate of incapacity is issued by a psychiatric facility in which an adult is residing or being treated, the Office of the Public Guardian and Trustee automatically becomes the guardian and trustee for that adult. However, even in these jurisdictions, the Public Guardian and Public Trustee will step down if a suitable family member or friend can be found who is willing to act as guardian and trustee.

If you are considering making an application to the court to have the Office of the Public Guardian and Public Trustee appointed for your elderly relative, you are strongly encouraged to telephone the Public Guardian and Trustee first to discuss the matter. On the one hand, do not assume that you are entitled to ask for the Public Guardian and Trustee to be appointed or that it will accept the appointment. On the other hand, if you believe that your situation is one in which the Public Guardian and Trustee are the appropriate guardian and trustee, do not assume that the appointment will be refused. You should describe the dependent adult's situation fully to the Public Guardian and Trustee (including all medical evidence) and explain why you think it would be the appropriate guardian and trustee. The Public Guardian and Trustee will not refuse your request unreasonably but it will want to know who else is a possible candidate to be guardian and trustee.

In any court application in which a request is made for the Public Guardian or Public Trustee to be appointed, the court will ask you to prove that you gave adequate notice of the court hearing to the Public Guardian and Trustee. In other words, the court will want to know that the Public Guardian and Trustee knows about your application and will give it a chance to say whether or not it accepts the appointment.

2. Family Members in Dispute

A situation in which the Public Guardian and Trustee will generally act as guardian and trustee is one in which family members of the elderly relative are having an ongoing dispute about something relating to the dependent adult. It could be a dispute about who gets to act as guardian or trustee, about who should get access or visiting rights to the elderly relative, or about financial transactions that have been done by a family member who is already acting as a trustee. It could be any dispute that cannot be resolved by the family members themselves.

In this case there might be more than one family member who is otherwise suitable to act and who is quite willing to act. However, it is not in the best interests of the elderly relative to be the source of family strife, not only because this is very stressful but also because rival siblings often try to force an elderly relative to pick sides in the dispute. In a case like this, it may well be that the only way to end the quarrel and reduce the subsequent stress on the dependent adult is to take the guardianship and trusteeship out of the hands of the bickering family members.

Also, it is not unusual that a person acting as trustee for a dependent adult who is under attack by his or her siblings and has to resort to court assistance will have his or her legal costs paid out of the elderly relative's money. Legal disputes cost money. Even though it is perfectly legitimate for a trustee's legal bills to be paid by the dependent adult if the subject matter of the legal fight is the dependent adult, an ongoing dispute could well lead to dissipation of the elderly relative's finances. In other words, the Public Guardian and Trustee will act as guardian and trustee for an elderly person in this situation if it will protect him or her from family strife and the wasting of his or her money on legal fees.

The fact that the Public Guardian and Trustee is a neutral third party able to stay out of family squabbles is generally seen as an advantage. The Public Guardian and Trustee employs professional, experienced guardians and trustees who know the law well so they do not make mistakes that cost the elderly relative money. They are also professional money managers. However, a disadvantage may be that an office full of strangers is not really able to provide the same sort of personal attention, affection, and interaction that could be expected if a family member acted as guardian and trustee. Whether or not the Public Guardian and Trustee is the right choice for your elderly relative is something that will be decided by you, the elderly relative, and a representative of the Public Guardian and Trustee.

3. What Does the Public Trustee Do As a Trustee?

If the Office of the Public Trustee is appointed as a trustee for your elderly relative, it will have the same authority as an individual trustee would have. There are some differences, given that the Public Trustee is a government office. For example, in jurisdictions in which trustees are required to post a bond, the Public Trustee is never required to post a bond or any other security before it is allowed to act as trustee.

If the Public Trustee were appointed as the trustee for your elderly relative, it could take all of the actions that an individual trustee, such as a family member, would take, such as selling property and paying bills. Keep in mind though that unlike a family member, the Public Trustee is not usually familiar with the elderly relative when it is first appointed as trustee. The Public Trustee will not know immediately whether your elderly relative owns a house and if so, who lives in it, whether there is a mortgage on it, or whether this year's property taxes have been paid. The Public Trustee will not know where your elderly relative banks, if he or she has an RRIF, or whether he or she owns a life insurance policy.

In order to know what needs to be done to look after your elderly relative, the Public Trustee must have access to information about the elderly relative. Some of this information may be supplied by you or other family members, particularly if one of you has been helping your elderly relative with banking or bill paying. However, once the Public Trustee has been appointed as trustee, it has the legal authority to go to the elderly relative's house, apartment, or long-term care facility room and look through private papers. The Public Trustee will be looking for important information such as insurance policies, bank statements, deeds to property, bills that need to be paid, and the elderly relative's will. You may be asked to arrange for the Public

Trustee to have access to your relative's home for this purpose.

The Public Trustee will take control of the elderly relative's money and property. It may close or move bank accounts. This is common practice, as the Public Trustee's job will be to protect the elderly relative's property and to maximize the estate. Investments may be cashed in or rolled over to new investments controlled by the Public Trustee. The elderly relative's money is invested so that interest is earned. Some of the elderly relative's possessions or home may be sold. If so, the money from the sale is added to the elderly relative's other money and is also invested.

The decisions about what to do with a dependent adult's money or assets, such as whether to close or move a bank account or renew an investment, are usually made by the Public Trustee without any input from family members. Its authority is complete and the Public Trustee is not required to seek permission from anyone.

When the Public Trustee acts as the trustee for an elderly person, the Public Trustee is, like all trustees, entitled to be paid for its services. Usually it will pay itself from the elderly relative's money, which is within its control. As with all trustees, the Public Trustee cannot pay itself without first obtaining court permission. Usually this permission is sought at the time the Public Trustee passes its accounts. The amount of payment allowed is set by the court.

If the Public Trustee is acting as the trustee for your elderly relative at the time that relative passes away, the Public Trustee's powers continue on uninterrupted until an executor (if there is a will) or administrator (if there is no will) of the elderly relative's estate is appointed. Once the executor or administrator is in place, the Public Trustee will hand over all of the elderly relative's property to that executor or administrator. It will also give the executor or administrator a full accounting of its activities as trustee, including all sales of property, all bills paid, all amounts paid to itself for fees, and all interest earned on investments.

4. Review of All Guardianship and Trusteeship Applications

Another function that is filled by the Office of the Public Guardian and Trustee in all areas of Canada is the review of all applications for guardianship and trusteeship. When you apply to the court to be appointed as a guardian or trustee for your elderly relative, you are required to serve a copy of your application on the Office of the Public Guardian and Trustee. Note that this applies to *all* applications, not just applications that ask for the Public Guardian and Trustee to be appointed. Refer to your provincial or territorial checklist to know at what stage you are to give the office notice. You will note that you have to give the office copies of everything, including affidavits and medical evidence.

When the Public Guardian and Trustee is served with your application, it will review the application to make sure that everything is in order. The following list includes what the Public Guardian and Trustee will be looking for:

- That all of the proper people have been given notice of your application.

- That the person who is applying to be guardian or trustee is the right person. For example, whether there is someone who is a closer relative that has a right to apply first, or whether there is a Power of Attorney or Health Care Directive signed by the elderly relative that names a person who would have the right to apply first.

- That all the needed documents are filed with the court and that there is nothing missing.

- That all the required medical evidence is included and that the medical evidence really does back up your claim that a guardian or trustee is needed for this particular elderly relative.

- Whether there is anything important missing in the information given (e.g., addresses, ages, relation to the elderly relative).

- That written consent from everyone whose consent is required has been included.

- That there are no objections to your application.

If the Office of the Public Guardian and Trustee has reviewed your application and has found that everything is in order, it will send a letter to you stating that the review has been done and that it has no problem with your application. The Public Guardian and Trustee will also send a letter to the court to let the judge know that your application has been reviewed.

4.1 If the Public Guardian and Trustee objects to your application

If the Public Guardian and Trustee finds something in your application that is out of place, this does not necessarily mean the end of your application, though there may be a delay. If the problem is simply that you forgot to take a certain step or that you made a mistake with your documents, this can be fixed. If it is something procedural, the Public Guardian and Trustee will tell you what the problem is. You can then fix the problem. For example, perhaps you forgot to include the medical report. If so, you can change your document to include the report, file the fixed document at the court, and give a copy to the Public Guardian and Trustee. If you can show the court that you fixed the problem, you will then be allowed to carry on with your application.

Sometimes the problem is not just paperwork. Sometimes the Public Guardian and Trustee will have a bigger concern. For example, it may believe that you are not the person with the right to apply to be guardian and trustee. If the Public Guardian and Trustee makes this kind of objection, again, this does not necessarily mean the end of your application. It does mean that the judge will follow up on the objection by asking you about it in court. Therefore if the Public Guardian and Trustee raises an objection to your application, you should take the comments seriously and try to put yourself in a position to meet its objection.

5. Ongoing Input

If you are appointed as a guardian or trustee or both, you will find that the Public Guardian and Trustee will still have something to say about how you conduct yourself. The Public Guardian and Trustee assists the court by reviewing your documents for future matters and giving the court its thoughts about the documents. In certain situations, the Public Guardian and Trustee will have input into what you do. You are required to serve copies of your documents on the Public Guardian and Trustee when you apply to the court to —

- renew your guardianship or trusteeship;

- pass your accounts (trustees only); and

- take specific actions such as selling real estate, winding up a business, or anything else that requires court permission.

6. Permission for Costs to Be Paid by the Crown

When you apply to be appointed as a guardian or trustee, there are costs involved in bringing that application to the court. For example, there are court fees, photocopying expenses, registered mail fees, and the time spent by you in preparing documents and appearing in court. Usually you will be asking the court for permission to repay those costs from the dependent adult's money so that you, as guardian or trustee, do not have to pay for it yourself. If your costs are reasonable, you should have no problem getting court permission for this.

It is also possible that the costs of the application can be paid by the Crown (*Crown* refers to the government) in certain circumstances. Those circumstances generally mean that neither the elderly relative nor his or her family is able to afford to make the court application. When there is a request that the Crown pay the costs, the request must first be given the permission of the Public Guardian and Trustee. In other words, the court will likely not order payment by the Crown without the consent of the Public Guardian and Trustee.

If you intend to ask that the costs be paid by the Crown, you will have to provide a sworn statement that it is a financial hardship for the dependent adult and his or her family to pay it. You may also be required to provide detailed financial information about income, expenses, and assets to back up that sworn statement.

7. Special Accounting Provisions

A passing of trustee's accounts is in most places done by the trustee directly to the court on a schedule determined by the court. With that kind of application, a copy of the affidavit that contains the accounting is served on the Office of the Public Guardian and Trustee, and it has the opportunity to give comments on the accounting to the court. However, the Public Guardian and Trustee has no other direct role in the passing of accounts.

This situation is different in British Columbia and Saskatchewan and is explained in the following sections.

7.1 British Columbia

The role of the Public Guardian and Trustee is different in one respect in British Columbia. The passing of accounts is done directly to the Office of the Public Guardian and Trustee. You provide your application and accounting information directly to the office and ask for approval of your transactions as trustee. If your accounts are in good order, you will receive a certificate from the Public Guardian and Trustee stating that your accounts have been passed. If the Public Guardian and Trustee has concerns about your accounting, it will then refer the matter to the court. You will then have to pass your accounts at the court, which is known as a Registrar's Passing of Accounts.

7.2 Saskatchewan

In Saskatchewan, once you are appointed as a trustee you must give an annual accounting and an annual inventory to the Public Guardian and Trustee. If all is well, the matter does not go to the court. If the accounts are not filed or the Public Guardian and Public Trustee has a concern, the accounting may then be referred to the court.

5

WHAT YOU NEED TO KNOW ABOUT GUARDIANSHIP

A guardian's role is not one of financial management; it is one that is concerned with the daily life, health, and safety of an elderly relative who is losing the ability to look after himself or herself. It is an interactive role that requires the guardian's attention, analysis, compassion, and time.

This chapter looks at who can and should be appointed as a guardian. This chapter also examines the powers available to a guardian and discusses the powers individually so that you can determine which of them are appropriate for your situation. This chapter includes the restrictions that are placed on guardians by law so that you can avoid making mistakes that lead to legal trouble.

1. Who Is Eligible to Be a Guardian?

Though it would be very convenient if the laws that apply to guardianship were the same everywhere in Canada, they are not. Canadian laws about guardianship are made by each province and territory and therefore vary across Canada. However, each area has one thing in common, which is that they set out a description of who may apply to be someone's guardian. The description varies from one province and territory to another and some areas give more detail than others.

The guidelines are set up to protect the elderly person who is vulnerable. You will note when reading the list below that even though the wording differs from place to place, the intent to protect the dependent adult is always expressed. The guidelines are generally not so strict as to exclude likely candidates for guardian.

As the requirements differ from one province and territory to another, the following is a summary of the qualifications that a person must have to apply to be a guardian in each area, taken from the laws of each province and territory. You will note that the various laws do not generally set out one set of qualifications for guardians and another for trustees. They are grouped together. Therefore this summary of qualifications applies to trustees as well as guardians. Use Table 4 to find the summary for your province or territory to determine whether you meet the basic guidelines as an appropriate guardian and/or trustee for your elderly relative.

The guidelines given here represent basic minimum standards that must be met. Meeting those guidelines does not give any individual person a right to be appointed, though it may give a right to make an application. Always remember that the courts which hear dependent adult applications have the authority to refuse your application whether or not you meet the basic minimum standards set out in the legislation, if the courts feel that it is in the best interests of the dependent adult to refuse it.

1.1 What does it mean to be in a position of conflict?

Some of the guidelines in Table 4 mention that a potential guardian or trustee cannot be in a position of conflict with the elderly relative. Even where this is not specifically stated in the law, conflict situations can become an issue and should be avoided.

Being in a position of conflict means that there is something about you or your relationship to the dependent adult that could mean that now or sometime in the future, you might have to choose between your duty to the dependent adult and your own best interests. Obviously a person in a conflict position is not a good choice as a guardian or trustee because it is only human nature to look out for your own interests, whereas the dependent adult needs someone who will wholeheartedly look out for him or her. It is important to understand that being in a conflict of interest position does not necessarily mean there is a problem existing right now. A person could have no issues at all with the dependent adult right now but still be in a conflict position if there is potential for conflict in the future. The following is an example of a possible position of conflict:

> A man owns a farm which he intends to leave equally to all three of his children when he dies. The man has a son who wants to own the farm himself and who has asked his father a number of times to sell the farm to him. Even though the father and son may get along well otherwise, the son could be in a conflict position in the future if he is made his father's trustee and has to decide whether or not to sell the farm. The conflict arises because the son will have to decide between what his father wants and what he himself wants.

Some relationships, by their very nature, may put the person in a conflict of interest. For example, a person whose job it is to provide personal care for a fee should probably not be the one who decides whether the dependent adult should have that kind of personal care.

Table 4
SUMMARY OF QUALIFICATIONS TO BE A GUARDIAN

Province or Territory	Qualifications for the Guardian
Alberta	• any person • must have reached age of majority • must consent to act • will act in the best interests of the dependent adult • is not in a position of conflict • suitable and able to act • must be resident of Alberta
British Columbia	• any person • must consent to act • must have reached age of majority
Manitoba	• any person • must give consent • must reside in Manitoba • must have reached age of majority
New Brunswick	• the wife or husband of the dependent adult, a relative by blood or affinity, or a friend or any other person who is concerned for the well-being of the dependent adult • must have reached age of majority • must give consent
Newfoundland and Labrador	• any person • must have reached age of majority • must give consent
Northwest Territories	• must have reached age of majority • must give consent • any person who has had friendly, personal contact with the dependent adult during the 12 months immediately before making the application • will act on behalf of the dependent adult • is not in a position of conflict • will be easily accessible to the dependent adult • is suitable and able to act • lives in the Northwest Territories

Table 4 — Continued

Northwest Territories — *continued*	**Note:** The court will give special consideration to the existence and closeness of the family relationship, if any, between the proposed guardian and the dependent adult. The court will also give special consideration to the wishes of the dependent adult, if the wishes can be ascertained.
Nova Scotia	• any person • must reside in Nova Scotia • must be of age of majority • must give consent
Nunavut	• must have reached age of majority • must consent • any person who has had friendly, personal contact with the dependent adult during the 12 months immediately before making the application • will act on behalf of the dependent adult • is not in a position of conflict • will be easily accessible to the dependent adult • is suitable and able to act • lives in Nunavut **Note:** The court will give special consideration to the existence and closeness of the family relationship, if any, between the proposed guardian and the dependent adult. The court will also give special consideration to the wishes of the dependent adult, if the wishes can be ascertained.
Ontario	• must either be a resident of Ontario or post a bond (the amount of the bond is in the discretion of the court and, in fact, the court may dispense with the bond altogether) • any person • cannot be someone who provides health care or residential social training or support services to the dependent adult for money, unless there is simply nobody else to apply • must be of the age of majority • must give consent
Prince Edward Island	• any interested person • must have reached the age of majority • must give consent

Table 4 — Continued

Saskatchewan	• any person who has a sufficient interest in the personal welfare of the dependent adult (for guardianship) • any person who has sufficient interest in the financial welfare of the dependent adult (for trusteeship, called *property guardian* in Saskatchewan)
Yukon	• any person • must have reached age of majority • agrees to comply with the duties of a guardian • suitable • the court will take the dependent adult's wishes into consideration

A business partner of the dependent adult may also be in a conflict of interest because if he or she has to choose what is best for the dependent adult, this might not be what is good for the business. You will have to think carefully about how your life interconnects with the dependent adult's life to determine whether your personal interests could conflict with this person.

Some relationships are specifically mentioned in the law as *not* automatically giving rise to a conflict of interest. For example, simply being a family member of the dependent adult does not automatically mean that you are in a conflict position. It is possible to be in a conflict position if you are a family member, but the family relationship alone is not enough to cause it. The following is an example of this type of conflict:

A woman might have lent her son $50,000 expecting him to pay it back when he is able to. Just the fact that he is her son does not put him in a conflict position should he become her trustee. However, the fact that he owes her a significant amount of

money is a potential conflict. His best interest (not repaying the money) would be in direct conflict with her best interest (repaying the money).

Also, if you are a beneficiary under the dependent adult's will, it does not automatically mean that you are in a conflict of interest position.

2. Who Would Be a Good Choice for Your Elderly Relative?

Everyone's situation is different so there is no one right answer for everyone. Guardians are generally chosen from among an individual's children, siblings, parents, or close friends. The best choice for any individual dependent adult will depend on who is available, who is suitable, and who is willing to take on the job.

Guardianship is an interactive role. It is not a case of signing papers occasionally and never seeing the dependent adult. When considering candidates for guardian, it is important to think about the geographical distance between the guardian and the dependent adult. The guardian cannot make day-to-day decisions in the dependent adult's best interest if the dependent adult has no opportunity to voice concerns or state preferences. Geographical distance can be a deciding factor if, for example, there are two children who are both willing to be the guardian of their parent, while one of the children lives in the same town as the parent and the other child lives hundreds of kilometres away. Remember that the ultimate deciding factor is what is in the best interests of the elderly relative, not what his or her children want.

It is quite common to see a husband or wife appointed as the guardian of his or her spouse if the spouse has suffered a stroke or a brain injury or is afflicted with Alzheimer's disease. This is often the case where the afflicted spouse is living in a hospital or long-term care facility and the other spouse is not. A spouse is a good choice because he or she is usually the person who knows the dependent adult the best. The spouse will know what activities interest the dependent adult, will know who should be invited to visit the dependent adult, and will have frequent interaction with the dependent adult.

You should consider the following questions when deciding who would be a good choice as a guardian for the elderly person:

- Is the guardian geographically close enough to do a proper job?

- Is the guardian frequently away on business or pleasure trips?

- Is the guardian already overwhelmed with other duties such as parenting or working?

- Is the guardian accessible to the dependent adult in emergencies or times of stress?

- Is the guardian trustworthy?

- Do the guardian and the dependent adult already have a compatible relationship?

- Is the guardian able to make important decisions without being unreasonably swayed by other family members?

- Has the dependent adult expressed a preference as to who the guardian should be?

3. Appointing Joint Guardians

It is possible for more than one person to be appointed as guardian, and this can work where the two individuals are able to get along well with each other and have similar ideas about the care that is in the best interests of the elderly person.

Sometimes it makes sense for more than one person to act as guardian for a dependent adult. Perhaps it is a situation where an elderly person has a number of children and more than one child is willing to help the parent. The children may feel that sharing the guardianship is a way of sharing the workload and responsibility as well as making sure that all the siblings are involved and informed of what is going on.

When there are two or more people appointed as guardians, they are referred to as joint guardians. Every decision made by them must be jointly made. This makes it essential that the joint guardians are able to communicate well, resolve disagreements constructively, and get along with each other. If the main reason two people want to act jointly is so that they can keep a suspicious eye on each other, there is a good chance the joint guardianship will not work.

The advantage to having joint guardians is that if one of the guardians should die or for some reason be unable to continue on as guardian, there is already someone in place who can carry on with guardianship without the court having to appoint someone new. There is also someone to help with the tough decisions. Decisions such as whether a parent should move to a long-term care facility can be very difficult to make. Invariably, the dependent adult's children who see him or her less frequently will disagree that the move is necessary and this will make it very hard on the care-taking child who has to persuade his or her siblings of the wisdom of the decision. Having at least one other sibling involved in the details of the dependent adult's care can be very helpful.

On occasion, a group of siblings are not able to agree on which one of them should be the guardian for their parent, so they all apply to the court together to have all of them appointed as joint guardians. This almost never works well. You are strongly cautioned against appointing more than two people, particularly people who do not get along with each other. Remember that when there is more than one guardian, all decisions must be unanimous. If a group of people is not even able to decide which of them should take on a particular task, they are almost certain not to be able to agree on health-care issues such as whether their parent should live in a certain long-term care facility, receive certain treatments, or be taken off life support. The more emotional the issue, the less able they will be to make rational group decisions. Working with a large group of people is cumbersome and almost always leads to disputes that have to be resolved by the courts.

4. Appointing an Alternate Guardian

A workable alternative to appointing more than one person at a time is to appoint one person (the *primary guardian*) and an alternate person who will step in if the primary guardian dies, moves away, or for any other reason cannot continue on as guardian. When the alternate guardian takes over, he or she will have all of the same power and authority that the primary guardian had. This works well in terms of costs because the alternate guardian can, when the primary guardian steps down, step into the shoes of the primary guardian without any court involvement.

It is important for the alternate guardian to understand that he or she has no authority at all to act as guardian while the primary guardian is acting. Being the alternate does not mean that the alternate is an *additional* guardian with equal authority. It means that he or she will only be the guardian if the primary guardian steps down, dies, or is removed from the position by the courts. In some jurisdictions an alternate guardian can act temporarily in the absence of the primary guardian, as long as the primary guardian has authorized this in writing. This might happen, for example, if the guardian was going on a lengthy vacation or having surgery with a long recovery time and did not expect to be able to properly fulfill his or her guardian duties. The time period of the primary guardian's absence should be clearly spelled out in writing before the alternate guardian takes over.

5. The Powers Given to Guardians by Law

Although the laws of the provinces and territories are made individually and are therefore not the same as each other, there are some similarities. The laws are formulated to address a certain situation, that of an elderly person who needs some assistance with daily living. Because of this, there are areas of overlap in terms of the specific powers or authority that guardians can be given by the court. For example, guardians everywhere in Canada can ask to be given the power to make decisions about the dependent adult's medical care. Each jurisdiction has a list of possible powers that a guardian can have.

In almost all jurisdictions, the laws governing dependent adults are written from the perspective that the guardians should be as unobtrusive as possible. Guardians should only give the help that is needed and not impose their actions on dependent adults in an inappropriate, restrictive, or controlling way. Because of this approach, the courts do not want to simply grant full guardianship with every possible power to everyone who applies. The court expects you to consider the powers that are available and relate them to the dependent adult with whom you are concerned. You should only be asking for the powers you really need.

In Ontario, for example, you can be granted full guardianship, in other words, with powers over all areas of the dependent adult's personal life and health care, only if you have convinced the court that the dependent adult is incapable in every single respect. As a result, most guardianship orders in Ontario are for partial guardianships.

Keep in mind that the judge has the power to deny your application, or to grant it only in part as he or she thinks is appropriate. You have to justify your request. The medical evidence that you gathered should help you decide which powers you need, as it should pinpoint specific problems (e.g., the dependent adult fails to take medication if not supervised). Your application is much more likely to be successful if the judge can see that you have put some real thought and consideration into what is needed to assist the dependent adult.

The laws of various provinces and territories across Canada give guardians the power to make decisions about the dependent adult's —

- living arrangements;

- engagement in social activities;

- ability to work and, if so, the nature or type of work and for whom he or she is to work;

- participation in educational, vocational, or other training;

- ability to apply for any licences or permits;

- legal proceedings that do not relate to the dependent adult's property;

- health care;

- normal day-to-day matters such as nutrition and hygiene;

- need to be physically restrained when necessary;

- commencement of a divorce proceeding on behalf of the dependent adult (subject to the restrictions set out in section 9 below);

- life support systems and consenting to withhold life support systems;

- termination of parental rights; and

- organ or tissue transplants.

In some jurisdictions, guardians are not required to pick and choose the appropriate powers but are simply granted status to take care of all related matters. Those jurisdictions are in the minority.

6. How to Know Which Powers You Should Request

As has been said a number of times in this book, each guardianship situation will be different because each dependent adult is different. In order to assist you in deciding which of the available powers you should ask for in your case, the following sections discuss some of the more common ways in which each of the available powers is used. The sections are not exhaustive but should give you some ideas about how to relate each power to your own situation. Proceed with the approach that you should not ask for anything you do not need right now and are not likely to need in the very near future.

6.1 The power to decide the dependent adult's living arrangements

This power is most often needed when the dependent adult may need to move from his or her usual residence into a long-term care facility. Somebody has to find, review, and choose the right facility and make arrangements for

consultations, evaluations, and the eventual move to the facility. Also, the facility will want to know who to contact if the dependent adult has a health-care emergency while he or she is living there, so the facility itself will want the dependent adult to have a decision maker in place. Over the last few years, care facilities have become much more insistent on this point and in many cases will not allow the dependent adult to move in until a decision maker has been appointed by the courts or by way of a Health Care Directive.

The decision about where a dependent adult should live is deceptively complicated. There are a wide variety of facilities available, and many of them provide different levels of assistance to the dependent adult. The facilities vary from hospitals that provide 24-hour care to assisted-living apartments that allow independent living with specified support such as laundry, cooking, or cleaning. It will be the job of the guardian to determine (along with guidance from the dependent adult's doctor, social worker, or other caregivers, if appropriate) which type of facility would be to the best advantage of the dependent adult. Once the initial placement has been made, the guardian must monitor the dependent adult's situation and abilities to ensure that the chosen facility continues to be the best choice.

Sometimes a guardian will be required to address an unusual situation in order to help the dependent adult. For example, there could be a relative, former spouse, or acquaintance of the dependent adult who threatens or frightens the dependent adult or consistently takes advantage of him or her. It would be up to the guardian to help the dependent adult find a living situation that was secure from that person and take steps to keep the dependent adult safe from that person. This situation would be covered by the power to decide where the dependent adult lives and with whom he or she lives.

6.2 The power to decide if the dependent adult will engage in social activities

Exercising this power is a combination of protecting the dependent adult and ensuring that he or she is able to live a rich life full of activities of interest to him or her.

If the dependent adult is capable of and interested in certain activities, it might be necessary for a guardian to ensure that the dependent adult is able to participate. For example, the dependent adult might require help in registering for a class or arranging transportation to a weekly card game, particularly if he or she is confined to a wheelchair. The dependent adult might need help getting a bus pass for getting to and from the coffee shop where he or she meets with friends. The guardian should do all that he or she can to help the dependent adult with the mechanics of his or her social life.

If the dependent adult would benefit from a social group or physical activity and is not getting enough interaction or exercise on his or her own initiative, the guardian would be called upon to find out what is of interest and benefit to the dependent adult and then arrange suitable activities. This might overlap with the power to decide where the dependent adult lives. For example, a dependent adult who lives in a small, isolated community and feels lonely or depressed might benefit from a move to a facility in a larger centre that offers access to a greater range of people and activities.

On the protection side, it would be up to the guardian to notice when certain individuals or groups of people have a negative effect on the dependent adult. For example, there could be someone who calls himself or herself a "companion" and lives in the dependent adult's home without paying rent or helping the dependent adult in any way. It would be up to the guardian to protect the dependent adult from unscrupulous persons who are taking advantage. Generally speaking, guardians who have the power to decide where the elderly relative live will also have the power to determine with whom the elderly relative will associate. This can mean the guardian will be able to restrict access to the elderly relative by certain individuals that the guardian feels should not have contact with the elderly person.

6.3 The power to decide if the dependent adult will work

The power in regards to a dependent adult's ability to work is not needed by the majority of guardians because most dependent adults have reached retirement age. However, if the dependent adult does work, it is up to the guardian to make sure that the workplace is appropriate and safe for the dependent adult and, depending on the individual's particular limitations, to ensure that the dependent adult is properly supervised. The guardian will have to ensure that the dependent adult is not being taken advantage of in terms of the type of work that is being done, the hours that are being worked, the wages that are being paid, and the working conditions that are provided. The guardian will also have to ensure that the dependent adult has reliable transportation, appropriate clothing, and access to water and nutritious lunch or snacks while at work.

These responsibilities are equally important whether the dependent adult is doing work for wages or is volunteering for charitable or social institutions. Many thousands of senior citizens who have retired from paying work like to participate in volunteer activities. Therefore, if you are considering becoming the guardian for a retired person who is involved in or who may become involved in arts, health, political, or community volunteer projects, you should ask for this power.

6.4 The power to decide the dependent adult's participation in educational, vocational, or other training

As with the previous power discussed, vocational training is rarely needed as most seniors are not involved in on-the-job training. However, the description of "educational, vocational, or other training" is quite broad. Not all education is taken for the purpose of getting a job and the dependent adult in your life may wish to attend classes to learn a new skill or hobby just for pleasure. It might also be the case that certain kinds of training are beneficial because they keep his or her mind sharp and body active.

6.5 The power to decide the dependent adult's ability to apply for any licences or permits

If the dependent adult still drives, or wants to continue driving, you should request this power. Remember that this is not just the power to allow the dependent adult to get a driver's licence but also the power to prevent

him or her from applying for one. This is frequently an issue as the independence afforded by driving is not something that many adults wish to give up, even when they can no longer safely drive a vehicle.

If the dependent adult carries on any business, profession, or trade, full time or part time, which requires a municipal business licence, you will need this power in order to renew licences as needed.

You may also need this power if renovations are likely to be done to the dependent adult's home or lot, as a building permit is probably required. In most jurisdictions permits are required for the building of decks, wheelchair ramps, and sheds, as well as paving of driveways.

If the dependent adult hunts or fishes, having this power will allow you to apply for those licences for him or her.

6.6 The power to deal with legal proceedings that do not relate to the dependent adult's property

Any legal matters that have to do with money or property, such as claiming an inheritance under an estate on behalf of the dependent adult or suing a person who injured them in a car accident are not the job of the guardian, but the trustee.

However, there are many potential legal issues that would be the job of the guardian to look after, should they arise. This would include any legal matter that is not related to money, such as —

- a dispute as to who should be the dependent adult's guardian;

- a question about who should have custody of, guardianship of, or access to a minor child or grandchild of the dependent adult;

- divorce;

- any proceedings about problems with health care, such as a facility that refused access, a question of whether a particular treatment should be undertaken, or a complaint about a hospital policy;

- recovery of the dependent adult's medical records; and

- a proceeding for legal name change, either of the dependent adult or a child of the dependent adult for whom the dependent adult would be required to give written consent.

6.7 The power to make decisions regarding health care

This power is almost always requested because it covers so many things that will need to be addressed for almost every dependent adult, including decisions about —

- surgery;

- treatment and whether it should be commenced, continued, or discontinued;

- the dependent adult undergoing certain medical or psychological tests, either with a general practitioner or a specialist;

- the doctor the dependent adult should see and how often he or she should see the doctor;

- particular aids to daily living that may be needed, such as a wheelchair, walker, hearing aid, glasses, special elevating bed, orthopedic shoes, or back support for chairs;.

- medications and if they should be tried, continued, or discontinued, whether refills are needed, and whether problems with medications (e.g., allergic reactions) should be addressed with a doctor;

- physiotherapy, massage, acupuncture, or other treatments that would benefit the dependent adult;

- psychotherapy and if it should be commenced or continued; and

- life support and if it should be discontinued if the dependent adult is in a vegetative state.

6.8 The power to decide normal day-to-day matters

The power to decide normal day-to-day matters such as nutrition and hygiene is almost always requested because it is a bit of a catch-all that covers so many different scenarios. When deciding whether you should request this power, ask yourself whether the dependent adult can do the following on his or her own, without assistance from anyone:

- Clothe himself or herself adequately and appropriately for hot or cold weather

- Plan and prepare appropriate meals

- Eat meals

- Manage toileting

- Bathe and/or shower

- Maintain good general hygiene (e.g., teeth, hair, skin)

- Do laundry or arrange for laundry services

6.9 The power to physically restrain the dependent adult when necessary

The power to physically restrain the dependent adult is not available in all jurisdictions, and when it is available (i.e., Northwest Territories, Nunavut, and Ontario), it should be used sparingly. This power should only be requested if the dependent adult is, has been in the past, or is likely to be in the future a danger to himself or herself or to others.

This might also be an appropriate power to request if the dependent adult has a habit of wandering away from home or getting lost, particularly if that habit coincides with memory loss that causes the dependent adult not to recognize familiar people. In such cases, it might be necessary to restrain the dependent adult, who may be uncooperative, in order to take him or her safely home.

7. Special Power of Purchase of Necessities

As you have seen a guardian has no authority to deal with the dependent adult's money; that is the responsibility of the trustee. However, some jurisdictions have a special provision in place that allows a guardian to buy essentials on behalf of the dependent adult without the consent of the dependent adult or his or her trustee. Essentials could include such things as food, shelter, weather-appropriate clothing, or medicine.

This power is put in place to ensure that the guardian of a dependent adult has the ability to keep the dependent adult safe and healthy and to carry out the duties imposed on him or her by the court. Allowing the guardian to buy essentials might be necessary if a trustee has not yet been appointed or is ill or travelling and is therefore not available. It could also be necessary if there is no trustee in place and the dependent adult is in charge of his or her own finances but is refusing or neglecting to pay for essentials.

This power is intended to be a temporary measure only, not a permanent arrangement. If the dependent adult continually refuses or neglects to pay for essentials on his or her own behalf, this person may need a trustee.

Once the guardian has purchased essentials for the dependent adult, he or she must be reimbursed by the dependent adult or the trustee.

8. Payment for Being a Guardian

While it is universally accepted that trustees should be paid for looking after the dependent adult's financial affairs, this is not the case with guardians. In many provinces and territories, a guardian is specifically prohibited by law from being paid any remuneration, compensation, fees, or allowance for the time and effort spent in looking after the dependent adult. In provinces where guardianship and trusteeship are combined into one role, this prohibition does not apply as there is no separation of which tasks are guardianship tasks and which are trusteeship tasks. (There are no territories in which guardianship and trusteeship are considered one role.)

Guardians are allowed to be reimbursed for reasonable out-of-pocket expenses. It is always a very good idea to keep receipts for anything you anticipate you will ask to be reimbursed.

9. Restrictions on Guardians

Earlier in this chapter, we looked at some of the areas of authority which are specifically set out in the laws across Canada. It is widely accepted that each of these powers is a general power that has to be interpreted and applied by different guardians to different situations. This means that there can still be some confusion as to what a guardian can or cannot do. Your court order may say that you can step into the shoes of the dependent adult and do for this person whatever he or she could do for himself or herself, but there are limits on a guardian's authority.

Not all restrictions on guardians' powers are specifically set out in the law of every jurisdiction. In some places they are codified law and in others the restrictions are the result of cases already heard in court that can be relied upon as precedents. If there is anything in the list below that you as a guardian are considering doing on behalf of a dependent adult, it is strongly recommended that you seek experienced legal advice before proceeding. Any one of these items could have a significant impact on the life of a dependent adult and his or her loved ones.

The following list includes some things that a guardian may *not* do on behalf of a dependent adult:

- Commit the person to a marriage

- Begin a divorce (except in Manitoba, Northwest Territories and Nunavut, where a divorce can be commenced with the specific permission of the court)

- Vote at any level of government

- Give the dependent adult's testimony in court

- Make a will (see Chapter 8 for more on this)

- Adopt a child or become guardian of a child

- Consent to medical treatment for the dependent adult for the primary purpose of medical research, if the treatment offers little or no potential benefit to the dependent adult

- Agree to an abortion

- Consent to sterilization that is not medically necessary for the protection of the dependent adult's health

6

HOW A COURT-ORDERED GUARDIANSHIP IS ENDED

Once you have been appointed guardian, there are a number of events that could bring your guardianship responsibilities to an end. The dependent adult could regain his or her capacity or could pass away. You might voluntarily step down as guardian due to ill health or so that someone else can take on the role. Always remember that you have been appointed by the court and, therefore, you cannot just quit and walk away from the job without the court's permission.

1. Removal of a Guardian by the Court

The court that appointed you as guardian can also remove you. Anyone who is concerned about the dependent adult and your actions as guardian can apply to the court to have you removed. The court will do so if it is in the best interests of the dependent adult (as opposed to the best interests of the person who is making the application, or your own best interests). In such cases, if the dependent adult still needs a guardian and you have been removed, the court will appoint another eligible person who agrees to act as guardian.

An application to remove you as guardian cannot be done without your knowledge. Any application to the court that concerns your actions as guardian must be served on you so that you have the opportunity to respond to what is being said against you. This is not only fair to you, but it is only common sense that you be involved to defend yourself if a person is accusing you of neglecting your job. If a person applies to the court to remove you and the judge sees that you are not present, he or she will question the applicant as to how and when you were served. If you were not served, the matter will be adjourned until you have been properly served.

You could be removed as guardian if the court found that you were not fulfilling your duties properly or that you were neglecting the dependent adult. For example, you might not be getting the dependent adult to his or her scheduled medical appointments or supervising his or her in-home assistance program. The person who is applying to the court to remove you will set out his or her allegations for the court and you will have the chance to respond to them. One missed medical appointment is hardly grounds for dismissal of the guardian, but a pattern of missed appointments could be.

Sometimes battles erupt within families, such as when two children of a dependent adult who dislike each other try to use visitation time with the dependent adult as a tool to upset the other sibling. A guardian can control who has access to the dependent adult and sometimes a guardian who is embroiled in a battle with a sibling will try to restrict access simply to win a battle without regard to whether the access itself is in the best interest of the dependent adult. Fighting of this kind is never good for the dependent adult and if it is ongoing, the court may appoint the Office of the Public Guardian instead of the person currently acting as guardian, because the Public Guardian will be a neutral party.

When a guardian is removed by the court, the removal (known as a *discharge*) is effective on the date stated in the order. If the order does not state a specific date, the discharge is effective on the day the order was granted.

2. Voluntarily Asking to Be Discharged

If you have been appointed by the court as the guardian for a dependent adult, it is possible to ask the court to discharge you from your duties. The court does not have to agree to your request, so you will have to give your reasons for wanting to be relieved of your duties. The following are some of the more common reasons that people ask to be discharged:

- The guardian's health is poor.
- The guardian is moving away from the jurisdiction.
- The guardian feels there is someone more appropriate to take on the role.

For example, a woman who is the guardian for her husband but whose own health is deteriorating due to her age may eventually want to hand guardianship of the husband over to her children.

If you are asking to be discharged, you have a much greater chance of success if you can line up a reasonable, willing replacement for yourself. This is necessary because if the dependent adult needs a guardian, it is certainly not in his or her best interest for the court to remove you without appointing a replacement. The court may want you to stay on until the replacement is found.

Normally, applications to be discharged are made during the regularly scheduled review applications rather than making a special court application just for the discharge question. It is always cheaper and more convenient to appear in court fewer times. However, it is possible to make an application to be discharged at any time if there is some urgency.

3. Death of a Guardian

If a court-appointed guardian dies, any alternate guardian that has also been appointed by the court will be entitled to immediately assume the role of guardian. This situation can continue without any confirmation of the court needed until the first court review period comes along. At that time, the alternate guardian who took over will advise the court of the death of the first guardian and the date on which the alternate guardian took over the role.

If there is no court-appointed alternate guardian in place, in most jurisdictions the Public Guardian would take over the role, either temporarily or permanently. Note that the Public Guardian will not be able to take on the role of guardian if they are not aware of the death of the court-appointed guardian, so it will be up to the executor of the guardian's estate to let the Public Guardian know about the situation.

If there is no alternate named but there is someone else among the dependent adult's circle of family and friends who is willing, able, and qualified to be appointed as the guardian, he or she should make an application as quickly as possible to become guardian.

4. Death of the Dependent Adult

The death of the elderly relative will immediately end a guardian's authority. A guardianship is only effective while the elderly relative is alive because the executor of the estate assumes authority once the dependent adult has died. See Chapter 17 for a more detailed discussion of what happens after a dependent adult dies.

7

WHAT YOU NEED TO KNOW ABOUT TRUSTEESHIP

A trustee is concerned with money and property, which means this person must be organized so that he or she can deal with all the paperwork properly. The trustee also has considerably more controls placed on him or her by law than a guardian does.

There are some general rules that any trustee must follow. These rules appear in the written law and common law of all Canadian jurisdictions. Simply stated, the rules say that the trustee —

- must always act in the best interests of the dependent adult,

- may not give away the dependent adult's money,

- may not use the dependent adult's money to support individuals other than the dependent adult and his or her dependants,

- may not use the dependent adult's money for the trustee's own purposes, and

- may not benefit from the dependent adult's property other than as the court allows.

This chapter will look at who is eligible to act as a trustee and what powers the trustee might be given. The chapter will also discuss the restrictions on trustees so that you have a better idea not just of what you may do, but what you may not do.

1. Residency Can Be an Issue When Applying to Be a Trustee

As with guardians, everyone who applies to become a trustee must have reached the age of majority and must consent in writing to act as a trustee. In some places, residency is an issue. In Alberta, Nunavut, and the Northwest Territories, the trustee must be resident in the province or territory in which he or she is applying to become a trustee. In Manitoba, a person who lives outside the province can only be appointed as trustee if the appointment makes him or her a joint trustee with someone who resides in Manitoba or with a trust company.

In British Columbia, Newfoundland, Ontario, and Saskatchewan, a person who lives outside the province can be appointed as a trustee, but the court in that province has the power to make the trustee post a bond for acting as trustee, if the court thinks that is appropriate. A bond is a type of guarantee that the person who is appointed as trustee will carry out the trustee's duties properly and diligently. When a person lives outside a particular province or territory, he or she also lives outside the jurisdiction of that province's courts, which would make it more difficult for the courts to control any dishonest or negligent behaviour by the trustee. Basically, posting a bond means putting up a sum of money that is returned to you if you carry out your trustee duties properly but which is forfeited if you do not carry them out. In deciding whether a bond is appropriate, the court will look at various risk factors such as the size of the dependent adult's estate, the amount of any debts, the relationship of the dependent adult and the trustee, the proximity of other family members and friends who can keep an eye on things, and the financial solidity of the trustee.

In New Brunswick, Nova Scotia, and Prince Edward Island, a person who lives outside of the province who is appointed as trustee automatically has to post a bond for acting as trustee. The court will decide how much the bond will be.

2. Who Would Be a Good Choice for Trustee?

Many of the criteria that apply to the choice of guardian also apply to the choice of trusteeship. For example, geographical proximity is important, as is being a person that your elderly relative knows and trusts. However, the kind of decisions made by a guardian are much different than those of a trustee and require a different set of skills. While a guardian must make decisions about such things as where a dependent adult will live and whether he or she needs to see a doctor, the trustee must make financial and possibly business decisions.

The following list includes some desirable qualities in a trustee:

- Ability and willingness to keep meticulous records

- Honesty

- Ability to work with and understand numbers

- Confidence and willingness to deal with realtors, investment advisors, appraisers, accountants, and lawyers as needed

- Ability to stay organized and on top of things

- Ability to budget appropriately and stick to it

- Ability to resist pressure from family and friends about how he or she is conducting the dependent adult's financial affairs

The majority of trustees take care of all of the record keeping. However, trustees do not have to do all of the bookkeeping themselves if the task is complicated and the dependent adult can afford to pay for help. For example, very few trustees actually complete the dependent adult's tax returns themselves — they hire accountants or tax preparers. Unless the trustee is particularly good at taxation, it would seem to be in the best interests of the dependent adult to have a professional hired to do the task properly. Late or incorrect returns can result in a financial loss including penalties and interest.

Some trustees also hire bookkeepers to update the records on a monthly or quarterly basis using bank statements and the trustee's receipts. Although a trustee cannot delegate any tasks that require judgment or discretion, it is all right to hire someone to do a specific task that is directed by the trustee. Always ask yourself whether it is reasonable to hire a bookkeeper or accountant on an ongoing basis, having regard to the —

- size of the dependent adult's estate,

- complexity of the property (i.e., does the dependent adult own companies, rental properties, foreign property),

- volume of paperwork and record keeping necessary, and

- dependent adult's ability to pay for this service.

People often wonder about conflicts of interest when choosing a trustee. The fact that the trustee is also the executor of the dependent adult's will is not a conflict. The fact that a trustee is the child, parent, spouse, or sibling of the dependent adult is not a conflict. There

is more information about conflict situations in Chapter 8, section 6.

As with choosing a guardian, the choice of trustee will be a matter of who is available, who is suitable, and who is willing to take on the task. It usually takes some thought and quite a bit of discussion among family members to come up with a viable solution that works not just for the dependent adult but for his or her loved ones as well.

3. Powers Given to Trustees by Law

The laws of each province and territory dictate the power and authority of trustees. As with guardianship, the laws differ in wording and sometimes in content from one jurisdiction to the next. Unlike guardianship, when you apply to become a trustee you are not always expected to pick and choose which powers and authorities you will need. Generally speaking, a trustee who is appointed by the court is authorized to take possession and control of all of the real and personal property of the dependent adult — with some restrictions. The order will rarely say that the trustee can manage, for example, the bank account but not the RRIF. The concept of trusteeship is that the dependent adult cannot manage financial affairs and the person put in place to assist him or her has the right and the obligation to manage all of the elderly person's financial affairs.

It is an opposite approach from guardianship. With guardianship, you get only the powers you specifically need and ask for. With trusteeship you get all the powers available unless there is some reason to restrict the powers.

Keep in mind that a court granting a trusteeship order can impose any limitations or conditions on the trustee that the judge feels are necessary or desirable in the circumstances, whether or not you have asked for the limitations or whether you agree with them.

For the vast majority of trustees, obtaining this standard blanket power is enough for their purposes. However, the court in most jurisdictions does maintain control of certain transactions that are not within a trustee's power unless the trustee has specifically asked for the court's permission. This means that if you, as trustee, want to take certain steps, even though you already have an order saying that you are the legal trustee, you have to go back to the court to ask for specific authorization to carry out the transaction.

This is an area in which many trustees run into trouble, as they generally believe, based on a layperson's reading of the wording of the court order, that they have unlimited authority with respect to all of the dependent adult's property. On the face of it, this may seem the case, but the judge has made the order within the framework of statutory restrictions that the layperson may not be familiar with. Trustees sometimes end up involved in transactions that they do not actually have the authority to handle, which causes legal trouble for themselves and for the dependent adult. Whether or not the trustees do have unlimited authority will depend in part on which province or territory issued the order appointing them as trustees.

For example, Alberta, Manitoba, Newfoundland, and the Yukon have a more conservative approach to trustee powers than the Northwest Territories and Saskatchewan. The following list includes some specific transactions in Alberta, Manitoba, Newfoundland, and the Yukon that a trustee appointed is *not* allowed to do unless he or she has provided the court with the full details of the transaction and received the court's permission to go ahead. There are other transactions mentioned in the legislation but these are the most commonly used provisions:

- Grant or accept a lease of more than three years

- Sell or dispose of property over a given monetary limit

- Carry on the dependent adult's business or trade

- Surrender a lease without accepting a new lease

- Compromise or settle a debt

These same powers are given automatically to trustees in the Northwest Territories. In other provinces, such as Saskatchewan, the powers listed above are not specifically listed in the legislation as being given to the trustee, but the trustee is given a blanket power to do everything that the dependent adult could do if he or she had capacity and there are no restrictions set out.

A power that requires court permission in Alberta and Manitoba only is the consent to the disposition of the homestead by the dependent adult's spouse. The homestead is any residence in which the elderly relative and his or her legally married (not common-law) spouse have resided. Also in Manitoba, the trustee may not settle a claim or lawsuit on behalf of the dependent adult without the approval of the court though he or she may do so in other provinces.

The situation is different again in Nova Scotia, where the only situation in which trustees must seek the specific permission of the courts is for the sale of real property.

Now that you are aware that these powers are given in some provinces and not others, and that in some places only some of the powers are given, you need to determine what exactly you are permitted to do as trustee where you live, and what you are not permitted to do. It is a good idea to read the act under which you were appointed as trustee. The act will set out your powers and the limits on those powers. If you are not sure which act applies to you, find your province or territory in the Checklist section of this book. The top of each checklist in that section sets out the appropriate act for each area.

4. Payment for Acting As a Trustee

A difficult question to answer is that of how much a trustee should be paid for his or her time, efforts, and responsibility as a trustee. Obviously not all trustees are paid the same, as some carry more responsibility than others or act as trustee for a longer time or have specific difficult circumstances to contend with. While all Canadian provinces and territories allow court-appointed trustees to be paid, some do not specifically give numbers or amounts of that payment. Many jurisdictions give a range of compensation that is available, but even those who do so refer to an amount of compensation that is *fair and reasonable*. This means there must always be a calculation of where any particular case falls within those guidelines.

In other words you are not going to be able to simply look up your payment on a chart. Nor is there any set hourly wage for trustees. Your compensation is going to have to be calculated within specific guidelines, if you are lucky, or within more general guidelines, depending on where you live.

The amount of compensation is always finalized or approved by a judge, who has the power to award the trustee more or less compensation than the trustee actually asked for. If your request is reasonable in light of the amount of work you have done and the amount of responsibility you have carried, you are likely to be successful with the request. The court recognizes that you should be paid a fair amount but at the same time, the court is interested in protecting the dependent adult's estate from being unnecessarily depleted. In British Columbia, the fees for a trustee (known as a *private committee*) are set by the Public Guardian and Trustee and approved by the court.

Therefore, what you have to do to claim compensation is as follows:

- Calculate the range of fees that is allowable for your province or territory based on the value of the assets you are looking after.

- Figure out where you fall within that range, based on the fair and reasonable factors set out in the next paragraph.

- When you have arrived at a specific amount within the range, you will ask the judge for permission to pay yourself that amount from the dependent adult's money.

When a court looks at what is fair and reasonable in any particular case, the court will consider the following factors. Read the list carefully and consider how each of them applies to your own situation:

- The length of the accounting period. A longer period of custodianship is more likely to warrant a larger fee than a shorter period of time.

- The full value of the property being looked after. The court will not want to deplete a smaller property by granting large fees. A larger property involves more responsibility.

- Any particular events that occurred during the accounting period, such as sale of the dependent adult's house, closing down of the dependent adult's business, settling of a lawsuit — having to look after those transactions will warrant a larger than usual fee because they involve more time, effort, and responsibility.

- The number of hours put in by the trustee on behalf of the dependent adult. More hours should translate into more compensation.

- The results being achieved by the trustee. A trustee who is sloppy or inaccurate with the accounts or who is losing money due to poor judgment is less likely to warrant a large fee than a trustee who is diligent.

- Whether there is any opposition to the request for the fee from family members of the dependent adult or other interested parties.

- The going rate for similar applications.

- How much of the work was delegated to other people. If you have done less work because you have delegated tasks to say, a bookkeeper, you can expect that to result in lower compensation.

4.1 Guidelines for Payment by Province or Territory

The following sections summarize the specific guidelines (or lack thereof) with respect to trustee compensation set out in the legislation of the various provinces and territories. If you simply cannot arrive at a dollar amount, you can always inquire at the Office of the Public Guardian and Trustee for information about what you should be charging in your specific case.

If there is more than one trustee for a dependent adult, the amount of fees allowed by the judge will be shared between the trustees. The shared portions are not necessarily equal. The division of the fees will depend on how much work or how many hours were put in by each trustee, and how much responsibility was carried by each of them. Usually the trustees have no trouble deciding on a division of fees that suits everyone.

In some parts of Canada, a judge may refuse to pay compensation to a trustee if the trustee is late with his or her review or passing of accounts application for no good reason.

4.1a Alberta

In Alberta the Trustee Act only refers to fair and reasonable fees. This province has a Suggested Fee Guideline that is normally applicable to executors of estates of deceased persons. The care and management portion of the Suggested Fee Guideline can also be applied to trustees of dependent adults' estates. The Guideline states that each year, a trustee can claim —

- 3/10 to 6/10 of 1 percent on the first $250,000 of capital,
- 2/10 to 5/10 of 1 percent of the next $250,000 of capital, and
- 1/10 to 4/10 of 1 percent of the balance of the capital.

4.1b British Columbia

Compensation in British Columbia is set at 5 percent of income from the assets, plus a set fee for asset management, annually. If you have done additional work that is out of the ordinary in any given trust year, you will have to describe this extra work in detail and request an additional fee. The actual amount of the fee will be set by the Office of the Public Guardian and Trustee.

4.1c Manitoba

Although Manitoba legislation does not set a monetary guide, it does say that when the court is deciding the amount of a trustee's fees, it will consider —

- the time spent and the kinds of duties performed by the trustee,
- the complexity of the dependent adult's financial affairs, and
- the rate at which fees are charged (i.e., is the fee requested based on an hourly rate or a percentage of the assets).

4.1d New Brunswick

The Trustees Act specifically applies to the trustee of a mentally incompetent person and simply says that the trustee is entitled to fair and reasonable allowance for his or her care, pains, trouble, and time expended.

4.1e Newfoundland and Labrador

The Mentally Disabled Persons' Estates Act does not set compensation for trustees. However, the Trustee Act allows a care and management fee for continuing trusts. The fee allowable is 1/250 of the average market value of the assets, per year.

4.1f Northwest Territories

A person appointed as a trustee is entitled to compensation (taken monthly, quarterly, or annually) from the estate of the represented person in accordance with the following:

- 2.5 percent on capital and income receipts,
- 2.5 percent on capital and income disbursements, and
- 2/5 of 1 percent on the annual average value of the assets as a care and management fee.

4.1g Nova Scotia

The Trustee Act in Nova Scotia refers only to fair and reasonable compensation.

4.1h Nunavut

A person appointed as a trustee is entitled to compensation (taken monthly, quarterly, or annually) from the estate of the represented person in accordance with the following:

- 2.5 percent on capital and income receipts,

- 2.5 percent on capital and income disbursements, and

- 2/5 of 1 percent on the annual average value of the assets as a care and management fee.

4.1i Ontario

Compensation in Ontario is set at —

- 3 percent of capital and income receipts,

- 3 percent of capital and income disbursements, and

- 3/5 of 1 percent on the annual average value of the assets as a care and management fee.

Trustees can also get an increase under section 40(3) of the Trustee Act.

4.1j Prince Edward Island

A trustee may claim no more than 5 percent of gross income on an annual basis plus 2/5 of 1 percent of capital annually.

4.1k Saskatchewan

The Trustee Act in Saskatchewan says that a trustee may request "fair and reasonable allowance for his or her pains, care, and trouble and his or her time expended."

4.1l Yukon

Compensation in the Yukon is set at no more than —

- 2.5 percent of funds received or disbursed, and

- 0.5 percent per year of the fair market value of the assets that the trustee is managing.

5. Personal Liability

Something that is not well known or well understood by individuals who apply to be trustees is that they can be held personally liable for financial losses to the dependent adult's property. For example, you might use the dependent adult's money to make a loan to someone but the money is never paid back. You might invest the dependent adult's money in a very questionable exploration venture that does not work out. You might sell assets, such as a house or car, for much less than fair market value. If you are fraudulent or negligent in dealing with the dependent adult's money or property under your control, you may be required to personally pay back the losses from your own resources.

For this reason, you should become as well-informed as possible before taking on the role of trustee. Then, while acting as trustee, continue to seek out information before making decisions. Chapter 8 of this book talks about some of the restrictions placed on trustees by law and you should become familiar with those restrictions.

Sometimes a trustee causes a financial loss to a dependent adult intentionally by using the money for a purpose he or she knows is inappropriate, such as using the money to finance the trustee's own luxurious lifestyle or pay off personal debts. However, this is not the norm. In most cases the loss is caused by a trustee who means well but has been careless or simply has not used common sense.

The following list includes some of the ways in which trustees have, intentionally or otherwise, caused a financial loss to a dependent adult:

- Not applying for a financial benefit to which the dependent adult is entitled, such as GST rebates or Old Age Security.

- Failing to file income tax returns for the dependent adult, thereby incurring penalties and interest on overdue taxes or causing the dependent adult to miss out on a tax refund.

- Failing to invest large sums of money by allowing the money to sit in a bank account earning negligible interest.

- Paying bills late so that interest is charged and late fees are incurred.

- Failing to keep up insurance on the house, household contents, car, or other valuables.

- Paying the trustee's own expenses or bills from the dependent adult's money.

- Borrowing money from the dependent adult for the trustee's own use.

- Investing the dependent adult's money in the trustee's business ventures.

As you can see, these are just common-sense ways of making sure that the dependent adult's money is not wasted and his or her income is maximized. Always remember that as a trustee, you are dealing with someone else's money and therefore you have to treat it more carefully than you would your own.

A comment frequently made by individuals who are trustees for their parents is that they expect to inherit the property one day anyway, so they feel they can treat it as their own. This is a very dangerous approach and one that is greatly frowned upon by the courts. Some children in this situation even go so far as to pay part of the dependent adult's money to themselves or sell property and keep the money, justifying all of this by saying they would inherit it one day anyway. This will always lead to trouble with the courts. As a trustee and fiduciary, you have to act in the best interest of the dependent adult even when you feel that best interest conflicts with your own. It is certainly not in the best interests of the dependent adult if you act as if you have already inherited property from him or her and can do as you please with it.

Provincial and territorial laws contain provisions that allow almost anyone who knows the dependent adult to intercede on the dependent adult's behalf if that person has reason to think that the trustee is not doing his or her job properly. It is most commonly another of the dependent adult's children (the non-trustee children) who notice that something is amiss, but it could be a neighbour, sibling, friend, or the Public Trustee.

When someone decides to intercede, he or she can bring an application to the court that forces the trustee to immediately account to the judge for all of the money and property he or she is managing. At that point, the judge will examine the trustee's ledgers, bank statements, and other financial statements to see whether there really is cause for concern. If the judge finds that money is missing or unaccounted for, he or she has the power to order the trustee to repay the missing money from his or her own funds. The judge may also discharge the trustee and/or order that no compensation shall be paid to the trustee.

Trustees are not held responsible for things that are beyond their control such as the general state of the world economy, a stock market crash, or a tsunami that destroys property. However, a trustee is held responsible for things that are within his or her control. A trustee is expected to behave reasonably and diligently in comparison to what any reasonable person would do in the same circumstances. Generally speaking, a trustee who is honest, careful, and reasonable will have nothing to worry about in terms of incurring personal liability.

The following are some specific ideas for avoiding personal liability:

- Read the order that appoints you so that you know what power and authority you have.

- Follow court directions and apply for your reviews on time.

- File income tax returns as required and on time.

- Pay the dependent adult's bills as they become due (automatic deposit and debit are good time-saving ideas).

- If you are selling real estate belonging to the dependent adult, get an independent appraisal from a qualified appraiser before accepting any offers so that you can establish why you set the price as you did.

- Shop around when making a major purchase and get written quotes. After the purchase is made, keep the receipt.

- Ask for court permission when it is required or recommended that you do so.

- Hire professionals (e.g., appraisers, lawyers, accountants) if you think you are in over your head.

- Insure real property and valuable personal property.

- Put valuable personal property such as jewellery in a safe place that is not accessible to other people.

- Do not mix the dependent adult's money with your own.

- Do not put the dependent adult's property in your own name.

- Do not use the dependent adult's money for your own use.

- Do not pay yourself a wage for time spent as trustee unless you are sure that you are specifically authorized by the court to do so.

- Be ready at all times to account to the court by keeping your records up to date.

- Respond to reasonable questions that are raised by other members of the family who are concerned about the dependent adult, as providing timely and accurate information can allay fears and concerns and prevent possible court applications.

RESTRICTIONS ON TRUSTEES' ACTIONS

A trustee who has control of a dependent adult's money or property is required to look after that property in a way that is to the benefit of the dependent adult. Because of the fiduciary relationship between the trustee and the dependent adult, the standard of care expected is quite high. While a trustee may behave irresponsibly, speculatively, or foolishly with his or her own money, the trustee is not entitled to do so with the dependent adult's money. While this kind of general guideline is important, sometimes it can be difficult to know for sure what specific actions you, as a trustee, are not permitted to do. Sometimes the general guidelines seem too vague.

To give some guidance about what not to do, this chapter will discuss some specific situations in which trustees are subject to restrictions. The following sections in this chapter discuss the authority given to a court-appointed trustee and the limits of that authority. It is a good idea to read this chapter before applying for a trusteeship, as it addresses some of the things that commonly go wrong with trusteeships.

1. Investments

A trustee who is managing a dependent adult's money is expected to invest that money wisely so that he or she makes the most of it. Provincial and territorial laws talk about investing and describe the expectations imposed on trustees. In each jurisdiction, the law requires trustees to use the "judgment and care that a person of prudence, discretion, and intelligence" would use in similar circumstances. While there are some variations on the wording, the concept that a trustee must invest reasonably and wisely (i.e., prudently) is expressed across the country.

This means that you cannot carelessly invest in foolish schemes. You will probably have to put some thought and perhaps some research into your decisions. If you do act foolishly with the dependent adult's money, you may be required by the court to pay back investment losses with your own money. This section of the book is designed to help you understand your limits as a trustee so that you do not incur personal liability.

Once you, as a trustee, are aware that you have to invest prudently, the question becomes how to achieve that. The Trustee Acts of Newfoundland and Labrador, Nova Scotia, Ontario, Prince Edward Island, and Saskatchewan offer some detailed advice intended to assist a trustee. In each act it says that a trustee must consider the following when deciding how to invest:

- General economic conditions

- Possible effects of inflation or deflation

- Expected tax consequences of investment decisions or strategies

- The role that each investment plays within the overall portfolio

- Expected total return from income and the appreciation of capital

- Need for liquidity, regularity of income, and preservation or appreciation of capital

- Assets' special relationships or special values, if any, to the purposes of the trust or to one or more of the beneficiaries

Other provinces give additional direction. For example, in Nova Scotia, the Trustee Act specifically directs trustees to diversify the portfolio of investments held for a dependent adult. It is definitely a good idea to read the law of your own province or territory so that you are fully informed as to what is expected of you. You may well be a trustee for many years. It is worthwhile to invest an hour or two in reading to ensure that your trusteeship runs smoothly.

If you are finding the details given for investing to be overwhelming, keep the following in mind. Generally speaking, if you have acted honestly, reasonably, and prudently with respect to the risks and rewards of any given investment strategy, you will not be liable for losses to the investments.

Given that you, as a trustee, must consider all of these factors and others set out in the law in your area, you may feel that you would like to hire a stockbroker, investment counsellor, or financial planner to help you manage the dependent adult's money. You may wish to put some of the dependent adult's money into mutual funds. This might not seem like a problem, particularly if you are used to investing your own money, but until very recently the law in most parts of Canada has not allowed trustees to rely on investment advisors or planners. Relying on advisors would mean that the trustee has delegated his or her decision-making power to someone else. Generally speaking, trustees are not allowed to delegate the powers the court has given them.

The law, however, is changing to allow trustees to delegate the care of investments. In some jurisdictions investment delegation is now allowed by law. In Alberta, British Columbia, New Brunswick, Nova Scotia, Prince Edward Island, and the Yukon, the law specifically says that the trustee can hire an agent such as a financial planner or investment counsellor. In Ontario and Saskatchewan, the law says that the trustee can get investment advice and is entitled to rely on the advice if it is reasonable. In Ontario, trustees are specifically authorized to invest in mutual funds and other pooled funds.

The laws in other parts of Canada do not specifically address the power to hire investment professionals, but they do talk about what kind of property a trustee may invest in. In the Northwest Territories, Nunavut, and the Yukon, a trustee is allowed to invest in "every kind of property, real, personal or mixed." In Newfoundland and Labrador, a trustee can invest in "any property."

Although the law addresses the situation differently in each province or territory, there is a general trend across the country towards loosening up the investment rules for trustees. The days when trustees were restricted to investments that guaranteed the capital seem to have disappeared as Canadians as a whole become more familiar with the stock market. Investing has become mainstream. Even in provinces where delegation to investment professionals is not specifically allowed, the fact that a trustee can invest in "any property" or "every kind of property, real, personal or mixed" most likely means that he or she is entitled to invest in bonds, stocks, mutual funds, and other items that normally are selected not by the trustee but by a hired agent. It would be a good idea in those provinces to ask a lawyer or investment professional to explain the rules of trustee investing to you before you release any of the dependent adult's money.

2. Trustee's Undertakings

An undertaking is a promise that carries legal consequences if it is not kept. In most Canadian jurisdictions, a person applying to become a trustee will be required to sign some form of Trustee's Undertaking. By signing the undertaking, the trustee is acknowledging the high standard of care that he or she is expected to uphold and he or she is agreeing to abide by the rules and standards imposed on trustees. Undertakings usually contain a list of actions that the trustee promises he or she will not do, such as using the dependent adult's money for his or her own purposes.

In some jurisdictions, such as Saskatchewan, the trustee is required to post a bond and may also be required to provide any sureties that the court directs. The bond generally replaces the need for a written undertaking as the bond is a form of insurance that the trustee will behave as promised.

3. The Dependent Adult's Will

A large number of Canadians have never made a will. Although there are no reliable statistics about how many Canadians have never gotten around to this task, everyone has friends and relatives who do not have a valid, up-to-date will. Therefore, it is not at all unusual for a trustee to be appointed only to find out that the dependent adult has not made a will.

This can be a problem, as dying without a will can and often does lead to delays, extra costs, and family disputes. The difficulty is that mental capacity is required to make a will, and a trustee is only appointed once the dependent adult has experienced a loss of some or all of his or her mental capacity. In other words, many dependent adults are simply no longer able to make a will. Sadly, it is not uncommon for a child of a dependent adult to insist that the dependent adult make a will that the child feels is favourable to the child, even if the dependent adult is no longer really able to deal with financial or legal matters. In fact, this is an area in which wills lawyers are trained to keep an eye out for elder abuse. If you make a will for the dependent adult and have him or her sign it, or if you take him or her to a lawyer who makes a will and has the dependent sign it, the will is only valid if the dependent adult has the required mental capacity.

This brings up the question of whether the trustee can legally make a will and sign it on behalf of the dependent adult. If you do not live in New Brunswick, you are not entitled to do so. A handful of jurisdictions specifically prohibit the making of a dependent adult's will by the trustee but most do not address it one way or the other in the legislation that allows for the appointment of trustees. Where there is no written law, we fall back on our common law, which means case law decided over the years. Canada's common-law approach to wills has always been that nobody can decide how a person's estate is to be distributed except that person himself or herself, because a will involves such a complex combination of wishes, intentions, and information known only to that person.

In New Brunswick, the law allows a trustee (called a *committee* in New Brunswick) to make, amend, or revoke a will on behalf of the dependent adult. However, taking this action is only legal if the committee's actions are then approved by the court. In other words, the committee is going to have to explain to the court why the will was set up the way it was, why changes were made, or why a will was destroyed. This allows the court to keep an eye on the committee and protect the

dependent adult. The court can disallow the will that the committee makes.

On the other end, some provinces specifically forbid a trustee to make a will for the dependent adult. In the Northwest Territories, Ontario, and Saskatchewan, the trustee is given the power to do anything with the dependent adult's estate that the dependent adult could do if he or she had mental capacity, other than make a will. The specific exception is clearly set out in the law.

3.1 Following the dependent adult's existing will

Sometimes a newly appointed trustee will find out that the dependent adult already has an existing, valid will. In most jurisdictions in Canada, the trustee is directed by law to try to find out whether the dependent adult has a will, and if he or she does, the trustee must do everything he or she can to work with that will while the dependent adult is alive. Even if this is not specifically directed in your jurisdiction, it certainly makes sense to follow that approach.

This means that a trustee should not, if he or she can avoid it, do anything that will disrupt the dependent adult's future plans for the estate. For example, the dependent adult might have a will in which he says that after he dies, he wants his daughters to have his antiques and his sons to have his tools. If possible, the trustee should avoid selling or giving away the antiques and the tools, because she knows they are destined to be gifts for the dependent adult's children.

Another situation in which the trustee might have to work with the dependent adult's will is that in which the dependent adult is moving from his or her family home into a long-term care facility. At that point in time, it is usually necessary for many years of accumulated belongings to be downsized to fit the dependent adult's new residence. There simply is not space to take all of the furniture, decorations, collections, and personal items with the dependent adult to a one-room living area.

If this case applied to the dependent adult mentioned earlier who wanted to leave his antiques and tools to his children, and if the dependent adult is not able to take the antiques and tools with him due to space restrictions, the trustee may consider giving the antiques and tools to the dependent adult's children in accordance with the will even though the dependent adult is still alive. The trustee must, however, consider whether the antiques and tools are likely to be needed to be sold for money for the dependent adult to live on.

This situation can seem like a no-win scenario for a trustee. On the one hand, giving the tools away while the dependent adult is still alive is considered giving away his property, which trustees are not supposed to do. On the other hand, selling the tools when the trustee knows the dependent adult wants his children to have them after his death is considered ignoring the dependent adult's wishes as expressed in his will, which the trustee is not supposed to do either.

The best way out of this quandary is to ask for court permission to give away the tools (or other property). If you can anticipate this situation arising, you can ask for court permission ahead of time.

If you do not anticipate the situation and have already given away the dependent adult's property in accordance with his or her will, you must make it clear to the court what has happened to that property. The best idea is to set out information about the gifts you have made at your first passing of accounts application and ask for the court's retroactive permission. There is no guarantee that you will get such retroactive permission because the courts would prefer that you ask before you act, but if property has already been disposed of, you will have no choice but to request it.

4. Using the Dependent Adult's Money to Support Others

Trustees are repeatedly told to make sure that they act only in the best interests of the dependent adult and not to spend the dependent adult's money on other people. This restriction is set out in the laws of many provinces and territories. However, real lives often seem too complicated for a simple rule like that to apply and sometimes questions arise about exactly who is supposed to be supported using the dependent adult's money. This section is intended to familiarize you with some of the guidelines for making your own situation work.

When a dependent adult is married, has children, or has other dependants, the trustee is automatically faced with the question of whether or not he or she can use the dependent adult's money or property for the benefit of those people. The rule about this is clear: the dependent adult's property can and should be used to support his or her legal dependants, just as the dependent adult would be obligated to do if he or she were still in charge of his or her financial affairs.

As mentioned above, real lives are sometimes complicated. It is not always easy to know for sure who is a *legal dependant* of someone else. As a general rule, a person's dependants are considered to be his or her spouse, children who are younger than the age of majority, and children who are older than the age of majority who have a handicap that prevents them from earning a living. Because of their status as dependants, they are entitled to continue to be supported by the dependent adult. For the trustee, this means that he or she can and should continue to support those individuals using the dependent adult's finances. People who do not fall within the definition of dependants given here are not automatically entitled to any financial benefit from the dependent adult but may, in some circumstances, be permitted to benefit. That is up to the court to decide.

When discussing who qualifies as a dependant, it is important to note that the word *spouse* does not only mean a legally married husband or wife of the dependent adult. Common-law spouses are equally entitled to financial support. It is not always obvious whether a dependent adult's romantic partner is actually a common-law spouse. In a situation where the dependent adult is in a long-term relationship or has had a child with the individual, it is relatively easy to determine whether the partner is the legal equivalent of a spouse. It can be trickier when relationships are of shorter duration.

There is no magic number of months or years that automatically qualifies a person to be considered a spouse for all purposes in all parts of Canada. For example, you may find that a person qualifies as a spouse under a pension plan within a month but must live with the dependent adult for a year to become a spouse for Canada Revenue Agency's purposes. In Alberta there is a unique law (the Adult Interdependent Relationships Act) which defines persons in either opposite-sex or same-sex relationships who live together for three years as spouses.

If you cannot determine whether a particular person in the dependent adult's life is a spouse, and you are worried about the consequences of allowing this person to receive a financial benefit, you must take steps to clarify the situation. You can consult a lawyer who deals with family law. Alternatively, you can at the time of your application present the judge with full information about the situation and ask for the court's guidance on the question.

Girlfriends and boyfriends who are not living with the dependent adult are generally not entitled to any financial benefit from the dependent's property. Neither are divorced spouses who have already completed their matrimonial property division.

When determining whether a child is a dependant, keep in mind that a child who has been legally adopted by the dependent adult has the same legal status as a child who was born to the dependent adult. Stepchildren who have not been adopted do not have the same status. As this book deals with adults who are losing their capacity due to aging, minor children are potentially less of an issue than spouses, though they should be mentioned in this day and age of blended families.

Sometimes the situation is even more complicated. There could be another person in the picture who is neither a spouse nor a child and would not normally be considered a dependant, such as the dependent adult's parent or sibling. In some cases, the person is living with the dependent adult or being fully or partially supported by him or her due to that individual's age, infirmity, or illness. In such case, discontinuing the financial support could be disastrous for that individual. However, your job as trustee is to act only on behalf of the dependent adult and doing otherwise could cause you to violate your duty as a fiduciary.

This can be a truly uncomfortable situation for the trustee. If you, as trustee, believe that the financial support to this person should continue, you should ask the court for permission for it to continue. For example, if the dependent adult's sister lives with him or her and is fully dependent on him or her because the sister has multiple sclerosis and cannot earn a living, it may be the case that the dependent adult feels a moral obligation to support the sister.

You should present the full facts of the situation (e.g., name, relationship, age, medical condition, the financial impact of the support) to the court. You would ask the court whether it is all right to carry on with the existing arrangements. The judge will consider all factors relevant to the situation including whether or not the dependent adult can afford to help his or her sister. Applying to the court will protect both the dependent adult and you.

Keep in mind that when you make an application to the court to find out whether any particular person should be supported by the dependent adult's money, you should remain as neutral as possible. In other words you should bring all applications to the court that truly require the assistance of a judge, even those applications which you personally may not approve of.

It is important for a trustee to realize that in a discussion about whether other people can derive a financial benefit from the dependent adult's property, the phrase *financial benefit* does not only refer to the direct transfer of cash. Giving someone money is an obvious example of giving a financial benefit, but it is not the only possible scenario. For example, a person who lives in the dependent adult's house without paying for room and board is receiving a financial benefit in the amount of the free room and board. A child of the dependent adult who is older than the age of majority but is attending college with the financial help of the dependent adult is receiving a financial benefit in the amount of tuition fees. Similarly, a person who uses the dependent adult's car without buying it outright, who has the dependent adult cosign a loan, or who accepts an extravagant wedding gift from the dependent adult also receives a financial benefit.

When you become a trustee, you have both a right and an obligation to investigate all current uses of the dependent adult's property and to discontinue arrangements that are inappropriate. This often causes upset and discord with individuals who will question your right to change what had been implemented when the dependent adult was in charge of his or her own affairs. No one likes change that adversely affects his or her income. The people who were supported by the dependent adult must be made to understand that you are acting on the authority of a court order.

Keep in mind, however, that if the dependent adult continues to have some capacity (as opposed to no capacity to deal with money at all) then you, as a trustee, are entitled to carry out the dependent adult's wishes. For example, if the dependent adult wants to give a wedding gift, then it is perfectly acceptable for him or her to do so, with your assistance. Remember that your trusteeship is to be carried out in the least restrictive manner possible. While the dependent adult can still make some financial decisions, you should assist him or her in those decisions.

5. Keeping the Trustee's Money Separate from the Dependent Adult's Money

It is essential that you do not mingle the dependent adult's money or property with your own. Most commonly, this happens by way of the dependent adult's money being put into a joint bank account or by way of the trustee's name (in his or her personal capacity) being added to the title to the dependent adult's home. Usually the justification given for taking these steps is along the lines of "it is easier for me to do the banking if it is in joint names." This is incorrect and tends not to be believed by the courts. It is just as easy to set up an account in the name of the dependent adult's trustee as it is in any other name and to use cheques or debit cards on that account.

Remember, you will need to report to the court on the dependent adult's financial affairs, which will be quite difficult to do if finances have been set up in such a way that it is difficult to determine which assets are owned by which people. Read Chapter 16 for more information about passing of accounts.

Another reason that money is not mingled is, of course, the protection of the dependent adult. Money that is put into joint accounts is considered to be owned by both of the joint owners. Therefore, setting up a joint account with yourself and the dependent adult is the same as giving all of the dependent adult's money to yourself. Obviously the courts are not going to allow that.

6. Conflict of Interest Situations

Conflicts of interest arise when a trustee takes an action in which, if things go wrong, he or she might have to choose between what works best for himself or herself and what works best for the dependent adult. The trustee always has to do what is fair for the dependent adult because he or she has a duty to protect the dependent adult.

6.1 The trustee buying property from the dependent adult

The trustee buying property from the dependent adult is a classic example of a conflict of interest situation because the trustee is, in effect, buying from himself or herself. It is specifically disallowed in many jurisdictions because of the potential for abuse. The trustee can only sell property to an arm's length purchaser for fair market value. This prevents the trustee from selling property to his or her spouse, children, or other relatives.

6.2 The trustee taking gifts or loans from the dependent adult

This is one of the most commonly breached rules of acting as a trustee and fiduciary. The rule, however, is very simple: taking a gift or loan from the dependent adult for yourself or for others should never be attempted without *first* getting approval from the court.

Getting the approval will involve preparing an affidavit in which you give the court the full facts about the loan and all of its terms and asking for permission to go ahead. Do not think of the court process as a rubber stamp because judges in general tend to be protective of dependent adults. Do not hide anything or forget to disclose material facts. If you borrow money from the dependent adult without court permission, you could be forced by the court to pay back the loan and could also be removed as trustee. If the court is particularly unhappy about the circumstances of the loan, you could also be ordered to pay the costs of the court application in which you were ordered to repay the loan or could be held in contempt of court.

7. Beneficiary Designations

If the dependent adult owns life insurance, RRSPs, RRIFs, or segregated funds, he or she will, at the time of purchasing that asset, have designated the beneficiary of the asset. This means that, for example, when the dependent adult bought life insurance he or she would have decided who is going to get the life insurance money when he or she dies. This person would have done the same with his or her RRSPs, RRIFs, LIRAs, and other funds.

Trustees are not allowed to change the designations on the dependent adult's assets and may be held liable for the full amount of the asset should they do so.

Beneficiary designations are considered by the courts to be testamentary in nature, meaning that they are the kind of wishes a person sets out in a will. This is because the dependent adult has decided already who is to get the value of the asset when he or she dies, making the decision similar to one in a will.

If you are acting as a trustee and a financial instrument of the dependent adult that has a beneficiary designation comes up for renewal, it is your responsibility to carry on that designation and not to make changes to it. With the help of a financial advisor, it is permissible to change the asset itself (e.g., from a low-interest GIC to a higher-yield mutual fund) but the beneficiary designation already on the asset must stay the same.

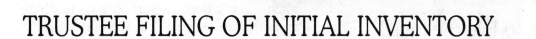

TRUSTEE FILING OF INITIAL INVENTORY

As the trustee, you are responsible for financial transactions regarding the dependent adult's money and property that take place while you are the trustee. You are not responsible for whatever the dependent adult did with his or her own property before you were appointed. Therefore, in order to know exactly what you are responsible for, in every jurisdiction, you must file an inventory that shows the court what you are dealing with. In this book, it will be referred to as an *initial inventory* to distinguish it from later inventories that may be prepared for other purposes.

All provinces and territories require an initial inventory to be filed. In British Columbia, the initial inventory is part of the Form 3 Affidavit that is filed at the commencement of the application. In Ontario and the Yukon, the inventory is filed as an integral part of the

management plan that is set up for the dependent person. A management plan is a document required to be filed by a trustee that includes a list of all assets and debts and describes what the trustee intends to do with each of them. For example, if the dependent adult owns a house, the trustee will state in the management plan whether the house is to be kept or sold.

The initial inventory shows all assets, debts, income sources, and expenses that exist at the time you take over as the trustee. It is intended to be a snapshot of the dependent adult's financial situation on the day you take control.

Once you have prepared the initial inventory, it is filed with the court and becomes part of the court's record. If you file the initial inventory and later find another asset that you did not know of at the time you made the initial inventory, you must file a supplementary inventory to advise the court of the new asset.

Initial inventories have to be *verified by oath* to be true and accurate. This means that you must prepare the initial inventory then attach it to an affidavit that you can swear before a Commissioner for Oaths before it is filed with the court. In jurisdictions in which the inventory is part of a management plan, the management plan itself is part of an affidavit.

1. When to File the Initial Inventory

In most but not all jurisdictions that require an initial inventory to be filed, the deadline is six months from the day the trustee was appointed. In Nova Scotia, it is three months unless the court says otherwise. You can file it earlier than the deadline, but should not file it later. This generous amount of time is allowed because the court recognizes that it is not necessarily easy to understand another person's financial situation quickly. Filling in the initial inventory might involve looking through the dependent adult's papers, talking to family members, calling or writing to banks and insurance companies, and checking with the Canada Revenue Agency (CRA) to see if tax returns have been filed. Therefore, enough time has been allowed for any needed investigations to take place.

Where the forms you need for the initial inventory have been prescribed by the Rules of Court of a province or territory, those forms are included in the Forms section on the CD. There is also a general inventory form that you can use if you live in a jurisdiction in which no particular form is required,

which you will find in the All Jurisdiction section of the CD.

2. Determining which Property to Include in the Initial Inventory

As a general rule, all property that is owned by the dependent adult should be included in the initial inventory. This may seem an obvious statement, but it becomes more difficult when you consider the various ways in which property can be held. This section will help you to properly identify and describe the property to be included in the initial inventory.

You must include the following in the initial inventory:

- All real and personal property that the dependent adult owns outright in his or her own name, whether or not that property has a loan or mortgage against it.

- The dependent adult's share of joint property. (See section 4 of this chapter for information about joint property and how to include it in your inventory.)

- Any property in which the dependent adult has a beneficial interest.

A beneficial interest is property that the dependent adult does not own directly but which will one day be paid to him or her. For example, the dependent adult might be named as the beneficiary of a life insurance policy or he might inherit money from a relative's estate. You would not include this property if the owner of the life insurance policy or the relative who left him the estate is still alive, because the owner could at any time change the beneficiary. However, if at the time you are doing your inventory, the person who owns the policy or the relative who owns the estate has died but the money has not yet been paid to the dependent adult, you should include it on the inventory as an account receivable.

The following list includes other examples of assets in which a person could have a beneficial interest:

- Any money held in trust, even if it is a trust for more than one person

- Money payable from a lawsuit, such as suing a person who caused a car accident that injured the dependent adult

- Dividends on investments

- Property that will be received as a result of a division of property in a divorce settlement

Millions of Canadians own RRSPs and RRIFs. Each person who owns an RRSP or an RRIF designates the name of a person who will inherit the money when he or she dies. It is quite likely that the dependent adult for whom you become trustee will own one. While the owner of this kind of financial instrument is still alive, he or she has control of the money and has the freedom to change the future beneficial owner. Therefore, when you are preparing an inventory for a dependent adult, make sure you include all RRSPs and RRIFs that belong to the dependent adult.

Term life insurance policies that are owned by the dependent adult are not included in the inventory unless the policy names the estate as the beneficiary. This is because no money is paid to anyone while the dependent adult is alive and therefore there is no monetary value to the dependent adult. If the beneficiary named is the estate, then money will flow into the dependent adult's estate after his or her death. Whole life policies that have a savings component may be included in the inventory if the dependent adult has in fact been using the policy to save money.

3. Determining the Value of the Property

The value you place on each asset and liability on the inventory must be the value of that item *on the day you became the trustee*, not the day you prepare the inventory. This is usually a different value because interest accumulates, pensions are deposited, and bills are paid in the interim. Remember that the whole point of the initial inventory is to describe what the dependent person owned *on the day you became the trustee*, not some earlier or later date.

For example, if you were appointed trustee on May 7, the dependent adult's bank account balance was $8,493.25. You do not prepare the inventory until you have had a chance to look at all the paperwork, which is on June 19. Between May 7 and June 19, the dependent adult received a pension cheque in the amount of $925.00 and interest in the amount of $2.74. In that time, you paid bills in the amounts of $78.02, $35.71, and $26.99. This means that on the day you prepare the inventory, the bank account balance is $9,280.27. On the inventory, you must show the bank account balance as $8,493.25 because that was the balance on the day you took control of the account. These transactions are illustrated in Sample 1.

Sample 1
LEDGER

Date	Item	Credit	Debit	Balance
May 7	balance forward	8,493.25		8,493.25
May 15	receipt of pension	925.00		9,418.25
May 20	phone bill		78.02	9,340.23
May 31	interest earned	2.74		9,342.97
June 10	utilities bill		35.71	9,307.26
June 15	groceries		26.99	9,280.27

It is impossible to overstate how important it is that you use the right value. The inventory that you prepare is the starting point for your trusteeship. The next step is for you to pass your accounts with the court, or upon the death of the dependent adult you account to his or her executor, and you will start with the values given on your initial inventory and show what has happened to each asset and debt. The numbers have to match or your accounts will not balance. If there is an error made, at some point it will have to be found and corrected. It is much easier to start off correctly than to try to find and correct an error later.

In determining the value of an asset shown on the inventory, always try to have a value given by a neutral, qualified third party to substantiate your determination. Remember that the values given in the inventory are placed in an affidavit that is sworn by you to be a true and accurate document. Do not simply pick a number that seems reasonable without some research or backup, unless there is simply no backup available.

The following sections give ideas on how to find or calculate the value of assets.

3.1 Real estate

It is not at all unusual for trustees to fill in an inventory without giving proper thought as to the values they are assigning to certain assets. It is essential that you do not simply pick a number that "sounds about right," particularly when you are dealing with real estate. If you fill in an inventory in which you say the dependent adult's house is worth approximately $350,000 but then six months later the house is sold for $275,000, how do you explain the difference to the judge who is reviewing your accounting?

The most reliable source of real property values is an appraisal given by a trained, qualified land appraiser. Less reliable but still acceptable is an estimate from an experienced realtor. When the dependent adult's estate is modest, generally the trustee will try to assign a value without paying the cost of an independent appraisal, which rules out the land appraiser. In such case, another acceptable (and free) source of property evaluation is the tax assessment notice issued every year by the city, town, or district in which the property is located.

The appraisal or estimate must be current. As a general rule, you should not rely on an appraisal or estimate that is more than three months old, particularly in markets where house prices are changing rapidly.

3.2 Mineral titles and leases

Mineral titles fall into two types — those that are producing revenue and those that are not producing revenue. For those titles that have not produced any revenue in the last five years, the value placed on them is likely only $1.00. It is impossible to tell whether mineral titles will begin producing revenue in the future, so it is impossible to base the value on possible future production.

For those mineral titles that are producing revenues, particularly those that have not been producing for very long, it is sometimes difficult to predict what the income will be in the future or for how long the title will continue to earn income. Therefore the value placed on the producing mineral title is an estimate. One accepted equation for finding the value is to multiply the current revenue by five years.

For example, with a mineral lease that produced income for the dependent adult of $4,000 in 2007 (the last full year) can be expressed as:

$$\$4,000 \text{ x } 5 \text{ years} = \$20,000$$

If the income from the mineral interest has been declining over the last few years and you believe that the income will continue to decrease, you might want to multiply the annual income by three years instead of five.

3.3 Vehicles

If you are a member of your provincial or territorial motor association, they will provide you with book values of vehicles upon request as part of your membership privileges. If you are not a member, look for advertisements for similar vehicles in the local newspaper. Make sure you look at current selling prices only. Another source of vehicle advertisements is a local magazine, usually published weekly, which is entirely dedicated to advertisements for vehicles being sold in that local area by private sellers, such as *Auto Trader* or *Bargain Finder*.

Look for vehicles of the same make, model, and year, preferably those with similar features and mileage.

3.4 Bank accounts, RRSPs, RRIFs, and portfolios

Note: This category includes portfolios that may have a mix of cash, stocks, shares, and mutual funds that are being managed by someone other than the trustee.

The holders (i.e., banks, trust companies, investment houses) of bank accounts, RRSPs, and RRIFs will provide you with a statement. Some statements are produced monthly, while others, such as long-term investments, are produced quarterly. The statement is your source of the asset's value. The trick is to make sure that you choose the right date. The closing balance of the statement is not necessarily the balance that applies to your inventory.

For example, using the bank account that was set out in section 3, the opening balance on May 7, was $8,493.25 and the closing balance on June 15, was $9,280.27. If you were appointed on May 25, neither of those balances is accurate. You would have to find out what the balance was on May 25. According to the bank statement, it would have been 9,340.23. (See Sample 1.)

Whenever you have statements that occur before and after the exact date you need and you simply have no paperwork that shows the day you need, always go with the balance on the earlier date.

3.5 GICs

Guaranteed Investment Certificates (GICs) have not been included in the previous category of assets because GICs and term deposits accrue interest, which is not payable until the GIC matures. A bank account earns interest too, but the bank usually pays the interest into the account every month.

To calculate the interest accrued on a GIC as of a certain date (that being the day you were appointed as trustee), use the following steps. As an example, we will use an inventory date of June 15, 2008. The GIC in our example has a principal amount of $5,000 and is earning interest at a rate of 2.2 percent per year. It was bought by the dependent adult on September 12, 2007.

Step 1: Multiply the principal by the interest percentage to find out the actual annual interest earned. For example:

$5,000.00 x 2.2% = $110.00 per year

Step 2: Divide the annual amount by 365 to find out how much interest is earned per day. Use 366 if it is a leap year. The interest earned each day is called a *per diem*. For example:

$110.00 ÷ 365 = .30 (30¢ per day)

Step 3: Figure out how many days of interest you should include. Normally the first day is the day the GIC was bought. If the bank has paid interest on the GIC since it was bought, the first day to be included is the day after interest was last paid. You can tell from looking at bank statements whether interest from the GIC has been paid. In our example, no interest has ever been paid. For example:

The days from September 12, 2007 (the day it was bought) to June 15, 2008 (the day the trustee was appointed) are 18 (September) + 31 (October) + 30 (November) + 31 (December) + 31 (January) + 28 (February) + 31 (March) + 30 (April) + 31 (May) + 15 (June) = 276 days.

Step 4: Multiply the number of days by the daily interest rate to find out how much interest has actually accrued on your GIC. For example:

276 days x .30 = $82.80

Step 5: Add the principal and interest together when you list the GIC on the inventory.

For example:

$5,000.00 + $82.80 = $5,082.80

3.6 Canada Savings Bonds

It is very quick and easy to find the value of Canada Savings Bonds because the government has provided an online calculator that is simple to use. Go to www.csb.gc.ca, choose your language, and on the right-hand side of the page, click where it says "Bond Values: Click here to check the value of your bonds." You need to know the bond series number to use this calculator.

3.7 Stocks and shares

This section refers to stocks and shares that are not held by a bank or financial advisor as part of a portfolio or RRIF. For example, you might find an original share certificate in the dependent adult's safe deposit box. Those shares must be evaluated individually. You will note from looking at the share certificate that the certificate is usually not just for one share; it can be for any number of shares.

If you know a stockbroker, you can ask for a quote from him or her. You will have to tell the broker the name of the share, the class of share, the number of shares and the date on which the value should be determined (i.e., the date you were appointed as trustee). The stockbroker may also ask you for the CUSIP (Committee on Uniform Securities Identification Procedures) number, which is an identifying number that will be printed on the original share certificate. Approaching a stockbroker may be the quickest and easiest route, though you may have to pay for the information.

Another alternative is to find this information yourself using either a newspaper or the Internet. Whichever source of information you choose, including the stockbroker, you will have to find out the price of one share then multiply that price by the number of shares.

If using a newspaper, the most comprehensive listing of shares is found in the *Financial Post*. Look for the section on stock quotes. Unless the shares you are hoping to evaluate are valueless, very old, or very obscure, you will likely find them listed in any daily city newspaper. For each share, newspapers show (among other things) the closing value of the shares on the day before the newspaper was published. Therefore, make sure you have the right day's paper before you start searching the columns. If you have the wrong day, you will get the wrong value. You want the paper that was published the day after you became the trustee.

Stocks and shares are not listed using their whole names. Each one that is traded on a stock exchange is given a symbol that is made up of three or four initials. For example, Stantec Inc. is called STN and Sears Canada Inc. is called SCC. You must know the symbol for any shares you are trying to look up. Once you know the symbol, find it in the alphabetical listing. Then look across the columns for that symbol. You will see a high and a low and possibly other information, but the value you need is the closing value.

If you do not know the symbol for the stock you are searching, you can easily find it online using a free website. To find a site, search "Canada stock quotes." Be sure to specify "Canada" as many sites show quotes in American dollars. Some suggestions are the Toronto Stock Exchange, Stockwatch, Globeinvestor, and Stockhouse.

On these sites, look for a feature that offers "symbol look up" and click on that. You will then be able to type in the name of the stock, which will help you locate the symbol for the stock. With any site you choose, make sure that you are being quoted Canadian dollars (this is usually done by choosing the Canadian exchange). If you search the Internet for stock quote sites, you will notice that many of the sites require you to sign on as a member before allowing you to search. As of the date of printing this book, none of the sites listed above require you to sign up as a member or charge a fee to search for quotes, and there are other similar sites available as well.

If you want to find the value of the shares using a website, you will have to know the symbol for the stock. Once you know that, you can type in the symbol and the site will give you a dollar value. That is the value of one share. The dollar value you are given will be the value of the share on the day you conduct your search, not the day you became trustee. Therefore to get the right value, you must find the place on the website where you can do a "historical" search. This will allow you to choose the date you want.

Once you know the value of one share, multiply that number by the number of shares to arrive at the total value of the share certificate.

3.8 Collections, antiques, and artwork

The only reliable way to put a value on unique items such as antiques is to ask someone who is trained and experienced with that type of asset for an appraisal. Even then, the value you are given will be an estimate. On your inventory, you want to name a fair market value, or in other words, the amount that asset would fetch on the open market if you sold it.

Collections are difficult to value, as it is impossible to place a value on the effort and time expended in researching, finding, and acquiring the individual pieces. Collections are generally valued as a sum of the individually valued pieces.

Coins and paper money are not necessarily given the value equivalent to the face value of the money. For example, an old $1.00 bill might be worth more than its face value of $1.00. The best way to find out is to take the

entire collection (or photographs and a detailed listing of it) to a specialist who will put a value on it for you. Similarly, stamps can be worth quite a bit more than their face value if they are rare or very old, and you should obtain an evaluation from a specialist.

This kind of specialist is not available in every Canadian town, so you may have to find one in the nearest large Canadian city using the Internet or Yellow Pages.

For hockey cards, sports photos, sports autographs, or other sports collectibles, it is a good idea to contact a shop which deals specifically in sports collectibles and memorabilia. If there is no such shop in your town, find one using the Internet or Yellow Pages, and be prepared to fax or email them a detailed list of the collection. Always remember to ask for prices in Canadian dollars if you are speaking with an American dealer.

Not all collections are valuable. Sometimes people collect things simply because they like them or find them interesting and there is no real monetary value to them. For example, people may collect thimbles, porcelain ducks, or teapots. There is little or no resale value, though they may have great sentimental value to the dependent adult who collected them. This kind of collection does not have to be given an independent value on the inventory, but can simply be included as part of the household and personal goods with a nominal value of $1.00.

Artwork can generally be evaluated by art dealers who operate galleries and shops. Not all galleries and shops handle all kinds of artwork. Artwork could range from Inuit carvings to oil paintings to pottery, and most galleries and shops specialize either by type of work or by artists from a geographic region. If the gallery near you cannot help you, ask for the name of a person or shop who deals in the type of artwork you need to value. Often framed paintings, prints, and photographs will bear a label on the back of them that identifies the shop at which they were purchased. That would be a good place to start.

You might also be able to find a website for an artist, if he or she is a commercial artist whose works are still circulating (e.g., Robert Bateman, whose prints are owned by thousands of Canadians). You might be able to find values for current similar works of art by the artist who created the works in the collection you are trying to value, or at least be directed to shops or galleries which sell his or her work.

The Internet can be a useful tool in finding values for unusual items. You may find a similar item for auction or sale on the website of an auction house or specialty shops. You could use that pricing as a guideline for the price you place on your inventory items. A note of caution: the price paid by an individual on any given day for an item on eBay or similar auction sites is not generally considered an accurate market value for similar items.

4. Joint Property

Joint property can be any asset, real or personal, that is owned by two people as joint tenants. The asset most commonly owned this way is a residence, particularly where the home is owned by a husband and wife. Other assets often held this way are bank accounts and some forms of investment such as bonds and GICs.

In law, joint property is not really owned half and half by joint owners. In fact, each of the joint owners legally owns the entire asset. This is why, when a joint owner of an asset dies, the surviving joint owner automatically owns the whole asset. However, for the purposes of completing an inventory on behalf of the dependent adult, you will have to think in terms of half and half.

When showing the dependent adult's interest in joint property you want to give the whole story. That is, you describe the whole property and clearly state that the dependent adult is a joint owner. Disclose the value of the entire asset then assign half the value to the dependent adult.

For example, take a case where the dependent adult and his wife own their home, which is worth $400,000, as joint tenants. Even though they own it jointly, meaning each of them would own the whole thing if the other one died first, you have to show half the value on the inventory because right now there are two owners. You would describe the asset giving the legal description of the property with a gross value of $400,000. You would then say that the dependent adult's share in the property is worth $200,000.

10

HOW TRUSTEESHIP IS ENDED

Because a trustee is appointed by the court, you do not have the option of simply quitting your job as trustee. You must have the court's permission to quit. When the court gives you permission to quit, it is referred to as *discharging the trustee*. Even if you decide to quit and walk away, if you have not been properly discharged by the court, you will still be liable for losses to the dependent adult's property.

Every time a trustee's job ends, whether it is because the trustee dies, the dependent adult dies, or someone else takes over the trustee's job, the trustee's accounts must be passed by the court.

1. Discharge of a Trustee by the Court

The court can release you from your role and responsibilities as trustee, either because you have asked to be released or because, even though you have not asked to be released, the court believes it is in the best interest of the dependent adult to release you as the trustee. The court's role is to protect the dependent adult and it will consider his or her needs above others. At the time you are discharged, the court is giving approval for what you have done so far and releasing you from further responsibility.

Being discharged by the court is instantaneous on the day the judge gives the order unless a specific date is chosen for accounting reasons. The latter situation is more unusual. As soon as the trustee is discharged, he or she has no more authority over the dependent adult's finances. In reality, there is usually a brief transition period during which the outgoing trustee will make arrangements with banks, investment houses, etc., to have his or her name removed from the dependent adult's affairs. Once he or she is discharged, the trustee cannot legally do anything on behalf of the dependent adult.

If you feel that you can no longer carry on with the job of trustee, you can ask the court to discharge you. You will have to explain your reasons to the judge's satisfaction. The following are the reasons most often given for a discharge request:

- The trustee's health is poor due to age, illness, or injury.

- It becomes a burden for the trustee to continue the job and usually he or she is no longer doing the job as well as someone else could do it.

- The trustee is moving out of the province or territory to take work elsewhere or to retire.

If you plan to ask the court to discharge you, you should, if at all possible, put together a proposal for alternate arrangements. In particular, you should arrange for someone else to act as trustee. Ideally, this would be the alternate trustee named in the order that appointed you. If no alternate was named in the order, you should make inquiries among family members and friends of the dependent adult who fit the legal requirements. You should obtain the new potential trustee's written consent and undertaking. You should then ask the court to appoint that person in your place. If there simply is nobody else who can and will act as trustee, you should contact the Office of the Public Trustee and let it know about the situation. Be aware that the judge does have the discretion to refuse the application to be discharged if he or she thinks that refusing is the best course of action.

It sometimes happens that a person other than the trustee will apply to the court to have the trustee discharged. The legislation of all jurisdictions in Canada allows for any person with a legitimate concern to apply to the court to compel the trustee to pass his or her accounts and possibly be discharged. However, this situation is relatively unusual, and is often the result of very poor communication between the trustee and a family member or friend of the dependent adult. While it is not unusual for family and friends to have questions or concerns about the trustee's actions, it is unusual for the situation to become so problematic that the court must become involved. The person making the application will have to prove to the court that the trustee is doing something against the dependent adult's best interests. If the court grants the application, the court will require the trustee to pass his or her accounts.

2. Passing of Accounts is Required

At the time you are discharged as the trustee, you must pass your accounts with the court, as you will be handing over financial control to another person. The judge will want to make sure that any discrepancies in the accounting are dealt with by the outgoing trustee and not carried over onto the new trustee. At this time, you should also make your proposal to the judge about how much you should be paid for having acted as the trustee. See Chapter 16 for instructions on how to pass a trustee's accounts.

3. Removal of a Trustee by the Court

Another possibility is that the court can discharge the trustee when nobody has made an application for the trustee's removal. The Incompetent Persons Act of Nova Scotia probably sums up the court's power the best when it says that a judge can, on his or her own initiative, remove a trustee if the trustee "removes from the province, becomes insane, or otherwise incapable of discharging his or her trust, is evidently unsuitable therefor, or is wasting the property of the [dependent adult]." While it is clear what "removing from the province" means, it is less obvious what being "evidently unsuitable" means. The judge has a lot of discretion to decide what it means in the context of any given dependent adult.

If the judge believes that you are not doing your job properly or that the dependent adult's welfare is at risk, the judge has the power to remove you as the trustee. This could happen if, for example, you are found to be helping yourself to the dependent adult's money, you are unable to explain large financial losses, you fail to pay the dependent adult's bills, or you neglect to apply to the court for reviews as required.

Generally speaking, your behaviour would have to be fairly egregious before the court would unilaterally remove you like that. For example, the court might discharge a trustee who failed to apply for reviews for ten years, but is unlikely to discharge a trustee simply for being late by ten days. The court is quite used to trustees who are new at the job, untrained in financial management, or unsophisticated in trust law. This does not mean that you can take your responsibilities lightly. It means that an honest, well-intentioned person who makes a mistake or is late with paperwork might be allowed some leeway by a court, but a fraudulent or negligent trustee should know that being removed from the job is a definite possibility.

In a situation where a judge feels it is necessary to remove a trustee for poor performance, the judge is highly unlikely to award any compensation to the trustee.

If a trustee is removed, either voluntarily or otherwise, the alternate trustee (if any) named in the order will step in and take over the trusteeship role. The alternate trustee will then have all of the powers, rights, and responsibilities of the original trustee.

4. Death of a Trustee

Obviously the death of the trustee brings an end to the trusteeship. As mentioned above, if there is an alternate trustee already named in the order, the alternate can take over the trusteeship seamlessly, without anyone having to apply to the court to appoint him or her. When the alternate trustee does that, he or she takes on the responsibilities of the earlier trustee and must do things such as apply for reviews on the date the first trustee had been ordered to do that.

As a deceased trustee cannot pass his or her accounts, the alternate trustee who took over will pass his or her own accounts at the normal time, indicating the date on which he or she took over.

When a trustee dies, the person who takes over as trustee must advise the Public Trustee in writing of the change in trusteeship.

11

HOW TO APPLY TO THE COURT FOR A NEW GUARDIANSHIP AND/OR TRUSTEESHIP

In some jurisdictions, a person cannot be appointed as a guardian and/or trustee for another adult without a court hearing in which the concerned parties show up in person to present their evidence and argue their case. The judge makes a decision based on what he or she sees and hears at that hearing and usually signs an order the same day. However, there are some jurisdictions in Canada in which nobody has to physically stand in front of the judge to present the case. Instead, the case is presented entirely in paper form. The evidence, including the medical reports, is given in the form of sworn affidavits. The judge reads the package of documents and if everything is to the judge's satisfaction, he or she will sign an order. The kind of court application that is done entirely on paper is called a *desk application*.

Refer to the checklist for your province or territory (included on the CD) for the details of your particular application. The forms and steps vary widely from one province to another. However, there are some similarities in the documentation of all jurisdictions. This chapter will provide you with a general overview of the purpose of the various documents you will need to use when you apply to the court to be appointed as the guardian or trustee for your elderly relative.

1. Application

The main document you will prepare and file is the application itself. It is called a petition in some jurisdictions. The purpose of this document is to summarize and describe what is going on in the court case. The application will do the following:

- Identify who is applying to the court

- Identify the dependent adult in question

- Describe exactly what is being applied for (e.g., guardianship, trusteeship, or both as well as any additional matters such as costs or bonds)

- Give a basic outline of the facts of the case

- Initiate a new court process, whether it is a desk application or a court hearing

- Identify which court will hear the matter (i.e., the level of court as well as the province or territory)

- Identify which Act or Rules of Court are being followed in the court case

The application is known as an *originating document* because it starts a new court matter. If you do not file an application, you cannot file any of the other documents as the application is the *start* of the court file. Once the application has been filed, you can later file more documents, such as supporting affidavits, bonds, or affidavits of service that are part of the same matter.

A form of application or petition for your Canadian jurisdiction can be found in the Forms section on the CD. When you are preparing an application, carefully check it to make sure it contains everything that is stated in the above bullet points. Sometimes where there is a blank space in a document, you might not be sure what goes in the blank space. Reading over the list above of what should be included might help you to spot something that has been left out and clarify what a certain blank space was intended to include. The CD also includes sample forms in PDF format with the instructions written in red font.

Your application must be signed by you but it is not required to be sworn before a Commissioner for Oaths. Your application must also be filed with the Clerk of the Court before you are allowed to use it in court. Chapter 12 contains quite a bit of information on filing documents with the Clerk of the Court.

2. Supporting Affidavit

In the application document already mentioned above, you have set out for the court a bare bones summary of what you are requesting. To show the court why you are making the request and to persuade the court to see your point of view in the matter, you need evidence. The evidence is given in a supporting affidavit.

An affidavit is a document that contains your testimony as well as documents and reports that are called *exhibits*. An affidavit must be sworn or affirmed before a Commissioner of Oaths or Notary Public before you will be allowed to use it in court. Chapter 13 gives more information on where to find a Commissioner for Oaths. All evidence given in a Canadian courtroom must be sworn or affirmed, even when it is written down in an affidavit and not given verbally. *Swearing* an affidavit means stating with your hand on the Bible that your evidence is true. *Affirming* an affidavit means promising that the information is true without reference to the Bible. Regardless of any moral consequences, the crime of lying under oath (whether swearing or affirming) is known as *perjury*.

Whenever you want to attach an item to your affidavit so that the item can be seen by a judge, the item becomes an exhibit. As you attach each one, give it a letter, starting with A. The next one would be B and so on. The exhibits are part of your document, so when you swear or affirm the document to be true you are also swearing that the content of the exhibits is true. Make sure that you attach *original* documents (not photocopies) as exhibits, except in the case where you simply have no way of getting hold of an original.

Each and every exhibit must be marked. That is, it must have stamped or printed on the face of it the following:

This is Exhibit "____" to the Affidavit of _____, sworn before me at the City of _____ in the Province/Territory of _____, this ____day of _____, 20___.

_____

A Commissioner for Oaths in and

For the Province/Territory of _____

You would fill in the blanks with the information that is appropriate to your case. You can fill in the exhibit letter and the name of the person whose affidavit the exhibits belong to before you go to see the Commissioner for Oaths. However, do not fill in the date of signing. The Commissioner for Oaths will do that on the day he or she commissions the affidavit.

The exhibit is marked on the front of the first page of each document. If the exhibit you are attaching is, say, three pages long, you only have to put the mark on the first page and not on pages two and three. While Commissioners for Oaths should be checking to

make sure each exhibit is marked and signed, it is always a good idea to double-check that none have been missed so that you do not have to come back to the Commissioner's office on a later day to fix an error.

The affidavit in question in your guardianship or trusteeship application is called a *supporting affidavit* because it gives the evidence that is needed to support or backup your application. The affidavit contains:

- Medical reports

- Consents of people involved

- Information about the dependent person, his or her medical, personal, and financial situation and the reasons he or she needs a guardian or trustee

- Information about you

- Your reasons for making the application, including your observations about your elderly relative

Although there will only be one originating application filed for each dependent adult, there may be more than one affidavit filed. In fact, it is quite common that a number of affidavits are filed during the course of a guardianship or trusteeship application. Some of the affidavits will be filed by you and some will be filed by other people. For example, in some parts of Canada, medical evidence is supplied by way of an affidavit given by a doctor. That would most likely be a separate affidavit from yours.

After the affidavits are sworn, all affidavits (yours as well as those of other people) must be filed with the Clerk of the Court before you can use them in court. Do not assume that affidavits prepared by others, such as medical doctors, are being filed on your behalf. Always check with the Clerk of the Court to make sure that documents prepared by others have been filed.

3. Consents

Whenever an application is made to appoint a guardian or trustee for an elderly person, there are certain people who must consent to the application going ahead. The following sections talk about some consents that are required in all provinces and territories, though in some places there are additional consents required as well. You generally do not have to obtain the consent of the elderly relative.

Consents can be given in two ways. With desk applications, the consent must be in writing because the person who is consenting will have no other opportunity to tell the judge how he or she feels about the application. Consents, once signed, are usually attached to the supporting affidavit given by the person making the application. Make sure you attach the original, signed and dated consent form and not just a photocopy.

The second way that consent can be given is verbally, but only in those parts of Canada where there is a court hearing held to decide whether a guardian or trustee should be appointed. A person who consents to the application can just show up in court and say that he or she consents, or can provide a written consent in advance.

If the person who is supposed to give consent either will not give it or simply does not get around to giving it, this does not necessarily mean the end of your application. If you can prove to the judge that you gave proper notice of the application (that being *all* of the relevant documents given to the person in

plenty of time for him or her to prepare for the hearing or desk application), you may still be able to go ahead. In such case, you can make the argument that the person knew of the application and had the opportunity to object to it if he or she chose to do so. This is one of the reasons why Affidavits of Service must be done in a timely manner.

3.1 Proposed guardian and/or trustee

The person who will be appointed as guardian and/or trustee of the elderly relative must consent in writing to be appointed and the consent has to be filed with the court. This is the case even when the person who will be appointed is the same person who is making the application. Consent of the person being appointed is something that is specifically set out as a requirement in law so it is never enough to assume that he or she has given consent, under any circumstances.

The CD contains consent forms for each jurisdiction.

3.2 Nearest or next nearest relative

The consent of the nearest relative of the elderly person is required. This refers to nearness in terms of relationship, not geographic nearness. If the nearest relative is already part of the application process because he or she will be appointed as guardian, alternate guardian, trustee, or alternate trustee, then you have to get consent of whoever is the next closest relative. For example, if you are applying to be the trustee for your widowed father, you are his nearest relative. However, because you are already involved as the applicant, you have to find the next nearest person. If you have no siblings, the next nearest relative is probably your uncle or aunt.

The nearest relative of any person is determined in the following order:

1. The person's spouse, whether it be a legally married or common-law spouse.

2. The person's children, both legitimate and illegitimate, naturally born and adopted, but not including non-adopted stepchildren. In most areas all children have an equal relationship in law with their parents, regardless of which child is older.

3. The person's parents, whether the person was born to them or adopted (but not stepparents who did not adopt the person).

4. The person's siblings of whole blood, including adopted siblings.

5. The person's grandparents.

6. The person's aunts and uncles.

Note that in some jurisdictions you are required to get the consent of only one person, that being the person who is the closest kin. In other areas, such as Manitoba and Nova Scotia, you are required to get the consents of all relatives who are closer in kin to the elderly relative than you are. As a general rule, it is better to get more consents than you need than fewer.

If you are required to obtain the consent of a person whose consent cannot be obtained because that person has passed away or lost capacity, do not simply ignore the requirement.

Add a clause to your affidavit to briefly explain why you could not obtain the consent.

4. Notice of Objection

In jurisdictions that allow desk applications, you will see on your checklist that you must prepare a Notice of Objection or Statement of Objection. You will treat this document differently than all others because although you make the document, you are mostly leaving it blank and you do not file it at the court.

The purpose of this document is to give someone a chance to object to your application. You will serve your application and affidavit along with your Notice of Objection on the people you are required by law to serve. (The checklist for each province and territory specifies who must be served.) The application and affidavit are fully completed, signed legal documents, but the Notice of Objection is not. If someone disagrees with your application, that person will take the blank Notice of Objection that you gave to him or her and will fill in the reasons for objection. The person will then file the Notice of Objection at the court. You are just giving the person a tool to use if he or she chooses to use it.

If nobody fills in and files a Notice of Objection, your application will proceed uninterrupted as a desk application, meaning that nobody has to appear in court. Usually there is a waiting period of ten days to allow for the filing of a Notice of Objection. The judge will proceed on the basis of the paperwork you have provided. However, if someone does file the Notice of Objection, there must be a court hearing date set down.

Obviously you do not know who is going to object or what the reasons might be for objecting. Therefore you cannot fill in the form. You have to leave it blank for the person to complete — all you need to fill in is the name of the dependent adult, the court which is dealing with the matter, your name, and a brief description of what is going on (i.e., an application to appoint you as guardian or trustee).

5. Know When to Consult a Lawyer

If someone formally raises an objection to your application, it means that a judge is going to have to hear arguments from you and from the person who is objecting so that the judge can make a decision about whether or not your application should be granted. This will require a hearing in which you will have to appear in a courtroom or judge's chambers and address the judge. Even if you have made a desk application, once there is an objection filed the desk application turns into an application that requires an open court hearing. At this point things can become more complicated. You will have to figure out the rules about presenting evidence. (For example: Is it given in affidavit form? Do you bring witnesses?)

In order to carry out the hearing successfully, you will have to know all the facts of your own case thoroughly, as well as all the reasons why your application should be granted. You may not know the person's reasons for objecting to your application until you actually appear in court, as not all jurisdictions require the objecting person to provide that specific information ahead of time. However, you may be able to guess at the issue if it is a family member who is objecting.

It is at this point that you should consider whether you need a lawyer to represent you at the hearing. Not everyone feels that he or she can address a judge in front of a room full of strangers. It can be intimidating. Some people may not feel that they can come up with the right arguments to defeat someone's objections. If you are having doubts about your own ability or desire to represent yourself, you may wish to consult a lawyer. If you do, make sure that you give the lawyer a few days' notice before the court hearing.

6. Orders

In most of the jurisdictions in Canada, preparing your application will include preparing an order that you will be asking the judge to sign. Always keep in mind that the order you are preparing is a request only. As stated earlier in this book, the court has the power to reject your application, grant your application, or grant it only in part. This means that the judge might cross out parts of your order at the time he or she signs it or might ask you to prepare a whole new one.

When you are preparing your order before your application, make sure that it includes everything that you need. If you forget to ask for part of what you meant to ask for, you cannot insert it yourself later or just assume that the judge would have agreed to it, had it been included. Never, under any circumstances, change an order after the judge has signed it.

The best way to make sure that your order is complete before the judge sees it is to double-check it against your application. Go through the application to make sure that it matches the order. Your order should include:

- A direction appointing someone as guardian and/or trustee, according to your application.

- Possibly a direction appointing an alternate guardian and/or trustee.

- A statement as to what powers the guardian or trustee will have.

- Possibly restrictions that are being placed on the guardian/trustee by the court.

- A deadline by which the order must be reviewed.

- A direction that an inventory be filed within six months (in all jurisdictions other than British Columbia and Nova Scotia).

- A direction with respect to bond or sureties, in applicable jurisdictions.

- A direction as to who is paying the costs of the application and in what amount.

The order will also have a place for the judge to sign and a place for the date of the order to be filled in.

12

FILING DOCUMENTS AT THE COURTHOUSE

Every application talked about in this book requires the filing of documents at the courthouse. This chapter will give you detailed information about how to do that and what to expect from the process. It is an important step, as making errors in filing can cause endless frustration and cause extra expenses to be incurred. It is recommended that you read this entire chapter on document filing before you attempt to file any documents.

Filing documents at the courthouse means that you are asking the court to open a new file to deal with your application. When you take your documents to the court, they will assign a file number. Make sure you write the number down because from that moment on, every document that has to do with your application *must* show that file number. It is also referred to as an *action number* or *case*

number. Court documents are not filed by a person's name, so referencing the number is vital.

You must give the court a copy of every document that is used in your application to become a guardian or trustee — your application for review and your application to pass accounts. If anyone else files a document on your application (e.g., Notice of Objection) the court will put that document in the same file as yours. In this way, the court will have a full record of everything that occurred in your application.

When you take a document to the courthouse, you will approach the counter and tell the Clerk of the Court that you want to file documents in a guardianship or trusteeship matter. Assuming that your documents are accepted for filing, you will be required to pay a court fee at that time. The fee varies across Canada. If you do not pay it, your documents will simply be given back to you, unused. Clerks of the Court deal every day with lawyers who are very conversant with the documents you are trying to use for the first time, but the Clerks are also quite used to non-lawyers. Make sure you ask for help or information if you need it.

1. Which Documents to File

Refer to the checklist for your province or territory to determine which documents you need to file with the court at various stages in your proceeding.

2. Where to Go to File the Documents

The checklists that accompany this book will tell you which level of court is the right one for you to file at. In all jurisdictions in Canada, this is done in the superior court (as opposed to the lower provincial or territorial court) except for Nunavut, which has one unified court. In small- to mid-sized communities, there is only one service counter in the courthouse that takes care of all superior court filing. In larger urban centres, you may find that certain matters, including dependent adult matters, are dealt with by a separate division of the superior court. In such case, you may be directed to take your documents to another service counter within the same courthouse.

Most provinces and territories are broken down by geographical areas, known as judicial districts. You are required to file your documents in the judicial district in which the dependent adult lives. If you do not know what the judicial districts are, you are likely in the right place if you simply take your documents to the courthouse that is geographically closest to where the dependent adult lives. Or, you could telephone the Clerk of the Court ahead of time and ask him or her to check on which judicial district you should be in.

3. Cost of Filing

Starting a new court file (or *action*) costs money. The fee varies across Canada, as set out below in Table 5. When you file your first document, you will have to pay the fee at the same time. You only pay the fee once and not every time you file subsequent documents, such as Affidavits of Service. Once you have paid the fee the first time, you can file as many documents as you need to file on that action without paying another fee. Courts will accept cash, debit cards, and sometimes credit cards. There is no GST payable on these fees.

When there is an existing dependent adult order and you apply to the court for a review or for a passing of accounts, you are not opening a new file action, even if it is several years later. You are using the existing action, as all documents pertain to the same dependent adult. This means that you do not need to pay a new file opening fee when you are applying for a review or passing of accounts.

4. Documents Rejected by the Clerk of the Court

It is important to note that the Clerk's job is not just to take your documents, regardless of their condition, and file them. The Clerk of the Court is required to look over your documents and if they are prepared incorrectly, to return them to you to be corrected. This helps

Table 5
INITIAL COURT FILING FEE

Province or Territory	Initial Fee
Alberta	$200
British Columbia	$208
Manitoba	$200
New Brunswick	$100
Newfoundland and Labrador	$60
Northwest Territories	$100
Nova Scotia	$215
Nunavut	$100
Ontario	$181 to $248
Prince Edward Island	$50
Saskatchewan	$130
Yukon	$140

prevent wasting the judge's time and creating a backlog in the courtroom due to unprepared applicants.

It is not at all unusual to have documents rejected by the clerk when they have been prepared by someone untrained in legal document preparation. As you can tell from looking over the forms that accompany this book, the forms can be complicated. Sometimes the forms are rejected more than once.

You can reduce your chances of having a document rejected by choosing the right checklist from this book and following it carefully. Meticulous preparation will also help. For example, when you are completing your documents, do not leave parts blank; if you do not know the answer to something, ask questions or do research until you find out. Follow

the document's headings so that you know what information goes where. Double check all figures by using an adding machine or calculator. Spelling does matter, particularly the spelling of names. Make sure that where witnesses to signatures are required, you have in fact had them witnessed. Formalities may not seem important but they must be complied with. Understand that if you do not take the right steps, such as filing and service of documents, your application will come to a stop.

Note that if you do not have access to a Commissioner for Oaths for the swearing of your documents, Clerks of the Court are Commissioners for Oaths and can assist you with that.

When you approach the service counter and hand over your documents for filing, the clerk will likely take a quick look at them to check for obvious deficiencies. For example, the clerk will check for:

- The original reports and that consents are attached

- Affidavits have been commissioned by a Commissioner for Oaths

- Exhibits are attached

- You have enough copies

- The document is signed in the right place by the right person

If the clerk thinks that your document can be filed, he or she will take the original and put a stamp on the back of it. The clerk will keep that document. This is the one that the judge will use. The clerk will also put a stamp on the back of one of your photocopies that shows the date it was received. This copy is for your records.

If the clerk points out any deficiencies to you and rejects your documents, make sure you understand what the problem is. It is up to you to correct these documents; the clerk will not do that for you. You cannot fix it if you do not understand what is wrong with it. Ask the clerk to point out exactly what the deficiency is and to explain it to you. Take notes so that you will remember it later, particularly if the clerk is referring to a law or rule number that you might want to look up. You will then be expected to fix the document and return to the courthouse at a later date with the new document for filing. If you do not fix the document, your file will never get to the judge.

You may think that if the clerk accepts your document at the counter and puts the stamp on it, your documents are fine. However, you may find that a few days later, the clerk sends it back to you by mail so that you can fix something that was not spotted at the counter when you filed it. This happens because at the counter, the clerk takes only a superficial look at your document to rule out obvious mistakes. Once the document is in the clerk's possession, he or she will go over it carefully line by line to ensure that it is perfect. If the clerk does send it back to you, he or she will include a form on which he or she will have checked off what needs to be amended. Again, you are expected to make the changes and return the new document to the clerk for filing.

SERVING THE DOCUMENTS

Service of documents on a person means that you give him or her copies of the documents. Each province and territory has slightly different rules for how and when service is to be done, but the purpose is the same everywhere. When you are starting an application to be appointed as the guardian and/or trustee for an elderly relative, you must, by law, let certain people know what you are doing. The documents are served on other people so that they will have notice of what you are doing and will have the chance to object to what you are doing.

Generally speaking, courts are very strict about ensuring that anyone who has the right to get notice of an application has in fact been served (see section 1 for more information about who to serve). Though it might feel like red tape to you at times, in guardianship matters, these requirements are in place to protect

the dependent adult. If you are unable to prove by way of Affidavit of Service that you served someone who has the right to be served, the judge may deny your application or refuse to hear your application until you have given proper service.

When you deal with service of documents there are two steps. The first is to actually serve the document. The second is to provide the court with proof that you served it. Both of these steps are discussed in detail in sections 3 and 4.

It is beyond the scope of this book to tell you everything there is to know about service of documents. There are other methods of service, such as service on somebody's lawyer or substitutional service that are not discussed here because they are usually not applicable to dependent adult situations. If you find that you must serve someone that you cannot find or for some other reason you cannot serve, it is a good idea to speak with a lawyer about the situation.

1. Who to Serve

The checklists provided in this book tell you who must be served by law. There are similarities in the requirements across the country. In all parts of Canada, the following people must be served with notice of your application:

- Dependent adult

- Dependent adult's nearest relative (see Chapter 11, section 3.2)

- Office of the Public Guardian or Public Trustee (depending on the application being made)

- Director of any institution in which the dependent adult lives, whether that be a hospital, hospice, long-term care facility, assisted-living facility, or group home

- Anyone named by the dependent adult under a power of attorney or health care directive

- Anyone who is going to be named as a guardian, trustee, alternate guardian, or alternate trustee who is not also the person making the application

Keep in mind, however, that sometimes it is not really very clear whether you should serve documents on a given person. For example, if the dependent adult lives in an institution, you generally have to serve the director of the institution. But if the dependent adult has an informal arrangement in which he or she lives in a private home with someone who acts as an informal caregiver (i.e., not appointed by the court) you might

not be sure whether you are supposed to serve documents on that caregiver or not. There could also be other people who are somehow involved in the dependent adult's life whose role is not clearly defined and you may not be sure whether you should serve them or not.

As a general rule, you are better off serving too many people than too few. You do not ever want to give the court the impression that you are deliberately avoiding service on someone for some reason. If you do give that impression, the court may think that you expect someone to object to your application and that you are trying to keep that person out of the picture to make things easier on yourself. If the court realizes that you have served too many people, this will not be held against you, as it shows that you are willing to involve others who may care about the dependent adult or have something constructive to add to the process of having a guardian or trustee appointed.

2. Service by Registered Mail

By far the most common method of service of documents on an individual is by way of registered mail. Note that some jurisdictions, such as Alberta, do not allow the dependent adult to be served this way, though all other parties can generally be served this way. Service of the documents takes place after the documents have been filed at the court. When you make the photocopies of the documents, make sure that you also copy the back of the document where the Clerk of the Court will have put a stamp. This shows the person you are serving that it is an existing court action and tells him or her the court file number so that if the person wants to, he or she can file a document in the action.

To serve by registered mail you will first prepare a letter to the person you want to serve. The All Jurisdictions section on the CD contains a form for this letter that you can adapt to your own use. In the letter, you state clearly that you are serving documents on the person. You put in a photocopy of each document that you are serving. Never put original documents in the letters; make sure you put in photocopies only and keep all originals for your own use. Sign and seal the letter.

Take the letter to the post office and request that it be sent by registered mail. Tell the postal clerk that the letter must be signed for when the addressee receives it. The postal clerk will give you a postal receipt, which is a piece of paper with a Canada Post stamp on it that shows the name and address you mailed to, shows the date, and shows a serial number for each letter. When you prepare your Affidavit of Service, this postal receipt will be your evidence that you mailed the letters. Mailing a letter this way, depending on how thick the enclosed documents are, will cost in the range of $4 to $6 per letter. Keep your receipts so that you can later be reimbursed for the cost.

3. Personal Service

Personal service usually means that a person is given the documents by hand. Service can be done by almost any adult, including a process server (person whose job it is to serve legal documents). In dependent adult matters, the dependent adult is usually served by a family member.

If you are going to serve the dependent adult, or another party, make sure that you have a copy of the documents that you can leave with him or her. You cannot just show the documents and then take them back; you must leave them with the dependent adult.

You must bring the documents to the attention of the party in question. Do not just slip the documents into the mailbox without saying anything. If you are with the person face to face and tell him or her that you have legal documents for him or her but the person refuses to physically take the documents from you, you can leave them on a table or in a mailbox at the person's residence. This is still good service.

There are no specific words that must be used, though you should tell the party that these are legal documents to do with an application to appoint a guardian or trustee for the dependent adult. You should also state that you are serving the documents on the person in question.

Although personal service on a dependent adult generally goes smoothly, there are cases in which it does not. If you are afraid that the dependent adult will react badly to the documents and possibly become violent towards you, make sure that you have another person with you who can protect you without harming the dependent adult. Remember that you only have to deliver the documents; you do not have to obtain a signature or get the person's consent. If you feel that the dependent adult might be less upset by having the documents delivered by another person or that another person might do a better job of explaining matters to the dependent adult, by all means have that person serve the documents. Alternatively, you can hire a process server.

A question that is raised frequently in dependent adult matters is whether a dependent adult still needs to be served when you are quite sure that he or she will not be able to understand it. This is not unusual, given that guardians and trustees are only appointed for adults whose capacity is to some extent diminished. The answer is that you do still have to serve the dependent adult unless the court dispenses with such service. It is not up to you to decide that service is not a good idea.

4. Proof of Service

When you give proof of service you must prove —

- which documents were served,

- who the documents were served on,

- how the documents were served (i.e., registered mail or personally),

- when the documents were served,

- where the documents were served (i.e., address), and

- who did the service.

If you have served documents by registered mail, your proof of service will be two pieces of paper. The first is the stamped registered receipt that the post office gives you when you send the mail. This proves how and when the service was done. The second is the signature of the person who received the registered mail. This proves who was served.

To obtain the second piece of evidence, a few days after you mail the letter, go to the Canada Post website. Look for the feature called "Track a Package" and type in the serial number that is shown on the postal receipt. A history of that letter's delivery will pop up. You will then be able to see when the letter was delivered, or attempts that were made to deliver the letter. Once the addressee has signed

for the letter, you will be able to view the signature (called the *signature acknowledgment*) online. Print the signature acknowledgment for each letter you sent. This might take more than one trip to the Canada Post website if the addressees do not pick up their registered mail right away. When you prepare your Affidavit of Service, the signature acknowledgments that you downloaded will be your evidence that the addressees received the documents you sent. They will be exhibits to your affidavit.

If you do not have access to the Internet to download these online signature acknowledgments, speak to a Canada Post clerk about how to obtain the signatures as proof of delivery.

When you have served documents by personal service, you may not have any physical proof that you served the documents. You may not have signatures, postal receipts, courier slips, or anything else that you can physically show the court to prove service. In these cases, your proof is your testimony that you served the documents. In other words, you will swear under oath or affirm that you served the documents and give the details of the service (e.g., where, when).

5. Preparing an Affidavit of Service

Proving service is generally done by way of an Affidavit of Service. An affidavit is a legal document that gives evidence that is sworn under oath. Therefore, an affidavit of service is a document that gives evidence about service of documents. If you are the person who served the documents, you will also be the person who swears the affidavit (also called the *deponent*).

The form of affidavit will vary from one province or territory to another, but the concept is always the same. The affidavit must contain copies of all of the documents that were served. They are stapled to the affidavit and once attached, are called exhibits to the affidavit. Each exhibit is assigned a letter, starting with "A." If you have postal receipts or signature acknowledgment cards, those are also attached as exhibits and are also assigned a letter.

For example, if you are Rashid Jones and you applying to become the trustee for your father, Ahmed Jones, you will have to serve a copy of your documents on the Office of the Public Trustee. You should have the following exhibits to attach to your affidavit of service:

- Copy of your application

- Copy of your affidavit

- Copy of any other documents that you were required to prepare as part of your application

- Postal receipt showing which day you sent your registered mail

- Signature acknowledgment card from the Office of the Public Trustee

Your affidavit of service might say, in part:

On October 9, 2008, I, Rashid Jones, served a copy of the application (attached as Exhibit "A") and supporting affidavit (attached as Exhibit "B") on the Office of the Public Trustee by placing the said documents into an envelope, addressing the envelope as follows:

Office of the Public Trustee
155 Carlton Street, Suite 500
Winnipeg MB R3C 5R9

and sending the envelope by registered mail.

Attached as Exhibit "C" is the postal receipt showing the date I sent the registered letter.

Attached as Exhibit "D" is the signature acknowledgment card signed by J.R. Smith of the Office of the Public Trustee.

Note that there are usually two affidavits of service on any application. One is the Affidavit of Personal Service on the dependent adult. The other is the Affidavit of Service by Registered Mail on all of the parties who were served by registered mail. You do not have to prepare a separate Affidavit of Service by Registered Mail for each person. You can make a list of them on one affidavit as long as you show the full name and address for each person.

14

WHAT TO DO AFTER THE ORDER IS GRANTED

After you have made your application to the court, you will eventually have an order of the court that appoints you as the guardian and/or trustee. Even if you prepared a form of order that you sent to the court for signing, the judge who decided your application may have made changes to it. Read the order carefully to make sure you know what it says. Your original order will be filed at the court as described in the next section, and you will be given a court certified copy or a court stamped copy. Anyone (e.g., bank or hospital) who asks for the order should be given a photocopy or notarized copy only, and you should retain the court certified copy.

1. Filing

If you have a court hearing, you will give the judge a form of order to sign, and if the judge signs it, you will have to file the order with the court. Filing it means that you are making the order an official part of the court record. If you do not file the order, you may not be able to rely on it or enforce it. Filing the order does not cost money, as there is already a court file in existence.

When you file your order, the court will keep the original document. This means that after the judge signs your order but before you file it, you will need to make at least one photocopy of the order. When the Clerk of the Court takes your original order for filing, he or she will put a stamp on the back of your photocopy (or photocopies) to show that the original was received by the court on the filing date. You can then make as many photocopies as you need of the stamped copy. In some jurisdictions, the Clerk of the Court will automatically certify one photocopy of the order for you at no charge.

If you have followed a desk application procedure, the copy of the order that you get should already have been filed before it was sent to you. To check, look on the back of the document, or on the top of the first page to see whether there is a court stamp on it that shows the date of filing. If you are not sure, you can always telephone the Clerk of the Court to ask.

2. Effective Date of Order

Unless otherwise stated in the order itself, the order takes effect on the day it was signed by the judge. The date normally appears right next to the judge's signature. That means that you became the guardian and/or trustee on the day it was signed. You are not responsible for financial transactions that occurred before this date or for personal decisions made for the dependent adult before this date.

3. Note Review Periods

Guardianship and trusteeship orders may have dates by which they must be reviewed. They are not expiry dates, but simply the date by which the judge wants the guardian or trustee to come back to court so that the court can review what has happened since the person was appointed. In Alberta, orders must be renewed after six years. In the Northwest Territories, it is three to five years. Read your order to find out when the order expires. It usually states in the order that the guardian or trustee must apply to the court for a *review* of the order by a certain date. A few months before the review date, if a guardian and/or trustee is still needed for the elderly relative, you should begin the review process to get a new order that extends the guardianship and/or trusteeship.

In some jurisdictions, reviews are only required when someone — the dependent adult, the Public Guardian or Trustee, or a concerned relative of the dependent adult — requests one.

In addition, trusteeship orders direct trustees to review their accounts with the court from time to time. Your order should say when you are expected to do your first review. For more information about reviews, see Chapter 15.

4. File Inventory

An inventory is only required to be filed when someone is appointed as a trustee or as a combination guardian/trustee. It is not required if a person is appointed as a guardian only. Chapter 9 of this book gives detailed instructions on when and how to file an inventory of the dependent adult's estate. The inventory establishes a starting date for your trusteeship and is generally due within six months of being appointed.

5. Costs of the Application

When you bring an application to the court to appoint a guardian and/or trustee, you are doing so for the benefit of the dependent adult, not for your own personal benefit. Therefore, it is appropriate that the cost of the court application be paid by the dependent adult and not personally by you. This is accepted practice.

The cost of bringing an application to court will include the initial fee you paid when you filed your documents as well as any other out-of-pocket expenses (e.g., photocopying charges and registered mail fees). Do not confuse getting costs with being paid for your time for being the guardian and trustee. You should not be charging for your time at this point in the proceedings, unless you have had to travel quite a distance to bring the application. At this point, all you are dealing with is the cost of getting yourself appointed.

Whatever you believe your costs to be, you should ask the court to grant you *costs*. This means that you are asking the court for permission for the dependent adult's money to be used to pay you back for your expenses. Ask for this at the same time you get appointed. Make your request by filling in the part of the order (near the end) that requests costs to be paid. You will be expected to fill in a specific amount and to state that it is to be paid by the dependent adult. If the judge agrees that you should be granted costs and if he or she agrees with the amount you have requested, the judge will sign the order. If the judge thinks you have asked for too much, he or she might still grant your order, but might reduce the amount you have asked for.

If you have not asked the court for costs and you are a trustee, do not expect to be repaid from the dependent adult's money. You may have access to accounts, but as a trustee, you cannot take any of the dependent adult's money for yourself without a court order (for more information on the restriction on trustees, see Chapter 8). If you have forgotten to ask for costs at the time you were appointed, you will have to wait until it is time to bring a review or passing of accounts.

If you have been appointed as guardian, you will have no access to the dependent adult's finances and so could not repay yourself in any event. However, if your order is only for guardianship and not for trusteeship, it is likely because the dependent adult still has the ability to deal with his or her own money. If that is the case, the dependent adult can simply pay you.

In some jurisdictions, there is a provision that costs of the application can be paid by the Crown (i.e., the government). This is generally only available when it would be a severe economic hardship on the dependent adult to have to pay the costs. To show that there is economic hardship, you will have to include a sworn statement about the hardship as part of your application. To find out whether the dependent adult you are concerned with would qualify for Crown aid, telephone the Office of the Public Trustee in the dependent person's area.

6. How to Use the Order with Institutions and Businesses

Once your order is issued by the court and filed, you should make several photocopies of it. Make one copy for each bank, investment advisor, tax department, hospital, long-term care facility, and other institution or place of business at which you will be representing the dependent adult. You will have to go to each of these places to let them know that there is a court order in place that gives you legal authority. In some cases you will be able to merely mail a copy to them. There is no need for any of the institutions or businesses to have the original court order; a photocopy will always be sufficient.

Some places will ask you for a *notarial* copy, which means the order has been verified by a Notary Public, or a *certified* copy, which means it has been verified by the Clerk of the Court that issued the order. Notarial copies are cheaper and easier to get. A surprisingly large number of banks, credit unions, and other places of business ask for a certified copy when they actually only need a notarial copy. When you are asked for a certified copy, you should ask whether it really does need to be certified by the court. You will usually find that it only needs to have a Notary Public stamp on it.

When you give a bank or place of business a copy of the order, you will be asked to provide personal details such as your full name, address, and telephone number. You will be asked to show your personal identification. This is because you have now stepped into the shoes of the dependent adult and assumed control over his or her affairs.

When using your order in a bank, it is extremely important that you keep the dependent adult's money and property separate from your own. Do not mingle your money and property with that of the dependent adult, even for a short time. You should change the name of the dependent adult's accounts so that you are the signing authority on the account. If the dependent adult is John Smith and you are Lucy Jones, the name of the account should be "Lucy Jones, trustee for John Smith." Do not depend on the bank to suggest the correct wording as the bank is not as familiar with the situation as you are. It is up to you to set the banking up correctly.

When setting up banking for a dependent adult based on a trustee order, do *not* —

- set up a joint account for yourself and the dependent adult,

- set up an account that shows you have power of attorney,

- change the dependent adult's account into your own name alone, or

- put anyone else's name on the account other than yours and the dependent adult.

If it is more convenient for you to move the dependent adult's bank account to a branch or even a different bank altogether that is easier for you to access, it is all right to do that. You may wish to look around at interest rates or customer services before deciding on where to bank. Depending on the abilities and independence of the dependent adult, you can work out with him or her whether he or she will have a debit card, a credit card, or be given a cash allowance. If the dependent adult, for example, likes to meet friends at Tim Horton's once a week, he or she will need a way to purchase coffee and perhaps transportation to and from the coffee shop. Follow the approach of placing the least amount of restriction on the dependent adult as possible while still protecting this person and his or her assets.

While at the bank, you may wish to arrange for the dependent adult's regular bills to be paid by automatic debit and for the account's statements to be sent to you. Keep in mind that one day you will be accounting to a judge for the money that went through this bank account under your watch.

Remember to send a copy of the order to places where the dependent adult might only do business once or twice a year, such as the local property tax authority and Canada Revenue Agency (CRA).

When you give a hospital or long-term care facility a copy of the order that appoints you as guardian, you will again be expected to provide personal and contact information. You will now be the person that will be telephoned if there is an emergency or a problem to be dealt with. If the doctors or caregivers believe that a certain treatment or medication would be beneficial to the dependent adult, it is you that will be asked to make the decision about whether or not to go ahead.

7. Serving Copies on Required Parties

After you have obtained your court order, make a photocopy of it for every person who was served with notice of the application — usually the dependent adult, the Public Trustee, the Public Guardian, the nearest relative, the alternate guardian/trustee, and the director of the institution where the dependent adult lives. Each of these parties must be given a copy of the order. It does not have to be certified or notarized.

It is not always required that service of the order be by registered mail. You can hand deliver it or send it by regular mail, if you choose. The benefit of using registered mail is that you will have proof of delivery should it ever be needed. (See Chapter 13 for more information about service.)

8. Read the Act

It is strongly recommended that once you are appointed as a guardian and/or trustee, you obtain a copy of the provincial or territorial legislation under which you were appointed, and read it in detail. This will give you important information about how you are expected to conduct yourself in your new role.

For example, the law in Northwest Territories directs that a guardian will seek to foster regular personal contact between the represented person (the dependent adult) and supportive family members and friends.

Keep in mind that one day you will be standing in front of a judge asking for a review of your performance as a guardian and/or trustee. The judge will expect you to know what your role involves. You are expected to take it upon yourself to teach yourself what you need to know to fulfill your responsibilities. The judge may ask you to give specific examples of how you fulfilled your role as set out in the law. It is best that you understand your role from the start. Reading the law may also help keep you out of trouble by letting you know specifically what you may not do.

To know which legislation to obtain, refer to the checklists on the CD for your province or territory. The laws (which may also be called *legislation*, *statutes*, or *acts*) are listed at the top of the checklist and the citation for each law is included to help you find it more easily. Once you know the name of the law, you can obtain it in one of several ways:

- Go to the Queen's Printer outlet in the nearest large city. The Queen's Printer is the official government supplier of the laws for each province and territory and it will sell you copies of what you need. The employees are generally very knowledgeable and will help you find what you need if you are uncertain.

- Go to the Queen's Printer website for your province or territory. You can then purchase the law you want with a credit card, download it, and print it.

- In the Northwest Territories, contact Canarctic Graphics to purchase a copy:

5108 – 50th Street
Box 2758
Yellowknife, NT X1A 2R1
Telephone: (867) 873-5924

- Go to a legal research site and find the law. One option is the Canadian Legal Information Institute (CanLII) at www.CanLII.org. The website operates as a free public legal research site managed by the Federation of Law Societies of Canada. Click on your province or territory, then click on "Statutes and Regulations." Under the list of statutes, click on the letter that corresponds to the first letter of the law you are looking for. For example, to find Ontario's Substitute Decisions Act, click on the letter "S." A list of laws starting with S will appear and you can scroll down the list to find the one you want. Click on it to read it. Once you find what you are looking for, you can download and/or print it for free. The acts of all provinces and territories can be found on CanLII, with the exception of British Columbia, which can be found at QP LegalEze (this site will charge you for the information).

9. Record Keeping for Guardians

One day you are going to be required to account for your guardianship and trusteeship to a judge. One of the smartest things you can do to make that accounting process run smoothly is to set up workable record-keeping from the very beginning. All records you keep as a guardian and/or trustee should be kept as up-to-date as possible, though they need not be elaborate or professionally prepared. You are allowed to hire a bookkeeper or accountant to help you if you feel you cannot manage the task by yourself, but you do not have to do so.

If you have the care of a person or his or her finances, or both, for a number of years, it will be impossible later on to reconstruct your records from memory. The key to achieving current, complete records is to set up a simple system that is not time consuming and that you will actually use on a regular basis.

A guardian keeps non-financial records. An easy and reliable method of keeping this kind of record is to purchase the sort of day planner or desk calendar that is used in offices to make appointments. This is a type of small book that has a separate page for each day. Each day is usually preprinted with the times of day in hourly or half-hourly increments. This kind of planner is available in all office supply stores (including online) and at bookstores. A day planner can reduce record keeping to a minimum while accurately storing all of the information you will need when it is time for a review.

In the day planner, do not write anything that does not pertain to the dependent adult. Devote the book entirely to the dependent person so that there is no sorting out to do later on. You do not have to write in the planner every day, in fact most days you will not write anything. Use the day planner to make appointments for the dependent adult to see the doctor, ophthalmologist, dentist, or physiotherapist. All you need to do is turn to the page with the right date, circle the time of the appointment, and write in the name of the medical professional the dependent adult will be seeing. You could add a short note, for example, next to an appointment with a doctor, you might write "to get flu shot," or "to get glucose test done."

Also record any other appointments to which you bring the dependent adult, such as a lawyer or an intake worker at a senior's facility. You do not need to write lengthy explanations of why you were there; a few notes as to the purpose or the results of the visit will do.

In addition to appointments, it is a good idea to make brief notes about any decisions you make on the dependent adult's behalf or changes that come about because of your actions. Keeping in mind that a judge will one day ask you exactly what you did as your relative's guardian, it would be extremely useful to have notes that record your activities, such as the day the dependent adult —

- moved to a new residence,

- had a particular surgery,

- began a new medication or therapy, and

- went to a special event or travelled.

10. Record Keeping for Trustees

Record keeping for trustees can be quite detailed, but again it does not have to be a time-consuming matter. Although there is generally a flurry of activity when a new trustee is first appointed, you will be able to simplify your systems so that you will actually be able to maintain them without a lot of work. Use automated features such as automatic payment of bills and automatic deposit of pension cheques whenever this service is available.

One item that every trustee will need is a daily ledger. Some trustees find it easiest to buy a notebook and keep records by hand as transactions occur, while others like to set up an accounting system on their home computers and record the transactions once a month using the bank statement. Many online bank statements can be downloaded to an accounting software system. You will be the best judge of which system is going to be both the most reliable and the most convenient for you.

Most jurisdictions in Canada do not require any particular form of ongoing record keeping, though the records do have to be consolidated into inventories from time to time when accounts are passed. There are some general record-keeping forms on the CD in the All Jurisdictions section that you can use if you wish.

11. Be Informed

Some provinces and territories have prepared manuals for use by people who have been appointed as guardians and/or trustees for the first time. Some manuals are available online. If the province or territory in which you live does not offer an online manual, try telephoning the Office of the Public Trustee or Public Guardian or the provincial or territorial Department of Justice to see whether they offer any booklets or other resources that you can obtain.

15

COURT REVIEWS

The court review is to ensure that guardians and trustees are only in place for as long as they are needed, but also to ensure that the individuals who are fulfilling those roles are doing a good job. A review basically examines the entire arrangement to see if it is working.

All orders appointing guardians and trustees are subject to being reviewed by the courts. In some parts of Canada the reviews occur at regular intervals and in other places, the reviews only occur when someone makes an application for a review.

It is important to realize that there is a difference between a review and a passing of accounts. A review means that the court is going to look at new medical evidence to see whether the dependent adult still needs assistance. It is going to look at the records and paperwork of the guardian and trustee to determine whether he or she is still the right person to act as guardian and trustee. It is going to look at the powers that were granted under the earlier order to see whether any powers need to be added or removed. A review is a complete examination of the entire guardianship and/or trusteeship order, and is almost like starting over from scratch. At the end of the review, the court gives an order as to who (if anyone) is going to be the guardian and trustee and which powers the person will have. Everything may continue on as it was before the review, or there may be changes.

Note: The passing of accounts is purely an examination of financial transactions. Obviously a trustee will apply for passing of accounts but a guardian will not, because a guardian does not handle the dependent adult's money or property. Chapter 16 delves into passing of accounts applications in much more detail.

In this book, there are separate procedural checklists for those provinces and territories where laws specifically set out a procedure for review. You can tell by a quick reference to Chapter 18 whether your jurisdiction has a separate checklist. In places where there is no specific procedure set out in the law, instructions are given on how to make a review application. All necessary forms are included or can be accessed through the CD.

1. Statutory Review Periods

The order that appointed you as guardian or trustee may contain a paragraph that tells you when the order has to be reviewed. Usually the dates given in the orders are based on provincial or territorial statutes that give a date by which the order must be reviewed. If the order that appoints you does not contain a review date, this does not necessarily mean that you will never have to participate in a review. It means simply that you will not have to participate in a review unless someone asks the court for a review or the court sees a reason on its own to direct you to carry out a review. This could happen at any time while you are a guardian and/or trustee.

In Alberta, orders of guardianship and trusteeship must be reviewed at least every six years. This provides some certainty and uniformity to guardians and trustees. However, even where a statute suggests a review date, the courts that grant guardianship and trusteeship orders have the authority to shorten or lengthen the review date as they see fit.

In the Northwest Territories and in Nunavut, a guardianship order must be reviewed between three and five years after it is granted. The actual time allowed will be set out in the order itself.

In Prince Edward Island, a guardianship order may be reviewed by a judge if an application is made for a review. This could be an application made by the guardian. Although the act does not state a specific time period, it is clear that the judge will "exercise continuing powers of review of the activities of the guardian."

In the Yukon, the act does not set a time deadline but describes a set of circumstances in which a guardian must apply for a review. To summarize those circumstances, a guardian must apply for a review if —

- the dependent adult's needs, circumstances, or ability to manage his or her affairs has changed significantly;

- the guardian's circumstances have changed in a way that reflects his or her suitability to be a guardian; or

- a conflict of interest arises between the dependent adult and his or her guardian.

Almost all jurisdictions in Canada allow for any person who is concerned about the dependent adult to apply to the court to compel the guardian or trustee to bring an application for a review. Therefore, even if you live in a jurisdiction that does not require you to bring review applications on a regular basis, you should always be prepared in case someone else requests the review.

2. New Medical Evidence Is Needed

When you apply to the court for a review, you will have to get new medical evidence. Keep in mind that the dependent adult's physical and mental condition may have changed, either for the better or for the worse, in the time that has gone by since you were first appointed as guardian or trustee. The court cannot make a decision about whether the dependent adult needs a guardian or trustee now based on medical evidence that is years out of date.

The requirements for medical evidence for the original application still apply to a review application. For example, if you needed two affidavits from doctors for your first application, you will again need two affidavits from doctors for your review application.

3. New Consents Are Needed

At the review application, one of the questions to be answered is, assuming the dependent adult still needs a guardian or trustee, whether the person currently acting in those roles is still the right person. In many cases, he or she is still the right person. However, sometimes a change is needed. Sometimes years pass from the first time a guardian or trustee is appointed for a dependent adult until it is time to review that order. In that time, a person who was appointed as a guardian or trustee may decide that he or she no longer wants to act as guardian or trustee. This could be because he or she has become ill, finds it to be too much work, or there is now somebody more suitable on the scene to act as guardian or trustee.

Regardless of the individual circumstances, whoever is going to act as guardian or trustee must sign a new consent form showing that he or she is consenting to act or to continue to act in that role. A consent signed for the initial application is not applicable to the review. You will have to get a new consent for the proposed guardian and/or trustee. You will also have to get consents from anyone to

be appointed as an alternate guardian or trustee.

4. How to Apply for a Review

Generally speaking, to begin the review process you will have to file an application and a supporting affidavit, much as you did to get a guardianship and trusteeship application in the first place. Consult the checklists included in this book for details about which documents and/or schedules you need to file. You will go through a very similar process and end up with a new order at the end of it all.

One difference is that in most jurisdictions, you will not have to pay a court fee to begin the review process. This is because you will not be starting a brand new court file. You will still be using the same court file because you are actually asking the court to look again at an order it made a few years ago.

You will have to go through the process of serving the documents on people just as you did when you got the guardianship and/or trusteeship in the first place, because it is important that the people around the dependent adult have a chance to see what is going on and to participate in the court process. You will have to serve all of the same parties. They are listed on the checklist for your area.

5. Documenting the Decisions Made by a Guardian

In order for the court to make a decision about whether or not you did a good job as a guardian and whether you should be reappointed for another term as guardian, the court will want to know what decisions you made and steps you took. A few jurisdictions have specific forms for you to report to the court about what you have done, but most do not. Even where there is a specified form, the information is put into an affidavit so that you can swear to the accuracy and fullness of the information. You will know whether there is a specified form for your area by referring to the appropriate checklist. Where no specific form is required, there is a suggested format in the forms given with this book that you can adapt to your specific circumstances.

The goal of this part of your application is to give *specific* information. It is not enough to give a general, blanket statement such as "I made all decisions that a guardian would normally make while I acted as guardian." Particularly where you are approaching the court without the assistance of a lawyer, the judge is going to want more specific information than that. You need to give details about what you decided on the dependent adult's behalf.

When you were appointed as a guardian, in most parts of Canada the order appointing you gave a list or description of the powers you were given under the order. For example, most guardians are given the power to decide where the dependent adult is to live. To report on your decision making, the best idea is to list each of the powers you were given and then describe how you used that power. In the example of having the power to decide where the dependent adult is to live, you might say:

I determined that the dependent adult was still able to live in her own home with some assistance. I made arrangements for grab bars to be installed in her bathroom and for a wheelchair ramp to be built at the home. I arranged for Meals on Wheels to deliver meals to her house six days a week and arranged that on the seventh

day of each week the dependent adult will spend the day with family members.

In some cases, where no changes were made to the status quo, your report could simply say:

I looked at all alternatives and determined that the best course of action was for the dependent adult to continue living in the same place.

Give the court a snapshot of what you have done for the dependent adult. If you have, for example, driven the dependent adult to medical appointments, taken him or her to the library once a week, taken him or her shopping for winter clothing, or helped him or her adopt a pet from the SPCA, describe those things briefly for the judge. Give a picture of what the dependent adult's life is like and show how you, as a guardian, have enhanced it.

Keep in mind that if you do not show the court that you have used or needed any particular power, the court may decide not to grant that specific power to you again on the review.

6. Documenting the Decisions Made by a Trustee

The decisions made by a trustee are included in some detail in the passing of accounts applications. Therefore it is not necessary to give a listing of decisions as you would do with a guardianship. In fact, most reviews of trusteeship orders are done in conjunction with a passing of accounts. However, as with guardianship, if you cannot demonstrate that certain powers or authorities are needed for you to assist your elderly relative, the unused powers may be removed by the court.

16

PASSING OF ACCOUNTS FOR TRUSTEES

Passing of accounts refers to the process of showing the court all of the transactions you have taken care of in your role as trustee. Guardians are not required to pass accounts because they do not handle money or property. This chapter refers only to individuals who have been granted authority by the court to deal with a dependent adult's money, real property, and personal property.

Passing of accounts, which is sometimes also called a *review of accounts* or simply an *accounting*, is done by way of an application to the court. You, as trustee, are applying for (i.e. asking for) the court to approve of how you have conducted the dependent adult's financial affairs. The financial records you give to the court are your *accounts* or your *accounting*. Your financial records are put into an affidavit, which you will swear to be true and accurate.

1. What the Passing of Accounts Shows the Court

There is more detail later in this chapter about what should be in your financial records, but the general idea is to give the court a full, honest picture of what you have done during the accounting period. The following sections explain what the court will be looking for in the passing of accounts.

1.1 Overall financial picture

The court will want to know whether the dependent adult's overall financial picture has improved or declined during the time you acted as trustee. State the actual difference in numbers. When you are first appointed as trustee, you will file an inventory of the dependent adult's property and debts. Use that as your starting point for the passing of accounts. You need to show what has happened with each of the assets on the inventory. For example, if a bank account that showed on the original inventory no longer exists because you decided the money would yield more income in the form of mutual funds, show the mutual funds in your accounting and explain the change. Show the current value of each asset and add any new assets that were acquired during the accounting period. Show what debts you have paid and any new debts that have been incurred.

Whether there has been an increase or a decrease in the total value of a dependent adult's property is not the only factor a judge will consider. However, it is a good starting point to show that the dependent adult's money is in capable hands.

To calculate the overall increase or decrease in the value of the dependent adult's property, use the Reconciliation of Accounts form in the All Jurisdictions section of the CD.

1.1a Increases in the dependent adult's finances

Explain any large increases in the value of the dependent adult's property. If, for example, the dependent adult's property was worth $110,000 when you began your trusteeship two years ago and now it is worth $130,000, you should be able to explain the increase of $20,000 to the judge. Generally a large increase is due to a one-time event such as an inheritance or an insurance settlement. If that is the case with your trusteeship, give the court brief particulars about what happened. Sometimes an increase is due to an upswing in the price of real estate. In other cases, a more modest increase can occur simply because a

trustee has managed the dependent adult's money in such a way that income now exceeds expenses.

1.1b Decreases in the dependent adult's finances

Explain any decreases in value of the dependent adult's property. It goes without saying that a judge is going to be more concerned about a decrease in the value of a dependent adult's property than he or she would be about an increase. However, a judge will not hold it against you if you have been managing the dependent adult's property in a reasonable, prudent manner and the loss is due to matters beyond your control, such as a market crash.

When there is a decrease in the dependent adult's property, if at all possible, show how you have contained or controlled the loss. For example, if a great deal of money was lost because a family member continually and inappropriately asked the dependent adult for cash handouts, tell the judge how you contained the situation by reducing the daily withdrawal limit on the dependent adult's bank card or removed credit cards from the dependent adult's possession.

1.2 Maximizing the dependent adult's financial situation

You will need to show the court that you have maximized the dependent adult's financial situation. One way of maximizing property is by looking into all possible sources of income available to the dependent adult. These might include federal government benefits, provincial or territorial government benefits, and any private pensions to which the dependent adult is entitled. You also want to show that you are making the most of any income-producing assets. For example, if the dependent adult owns a revenue property, you want to show that you have leased the property at all times for a reasonable rent and that you are collecting the rent. You also want to show that large sums of money are invested in such a way as to maximize returns.

1.3 Use of the dependent adult's property

Show the court that the dependent adult's property is being used only for those entitled to be supported by him or her, including his or her spouse, minor children, and children who are older than the age of majority but are prevented from earning a living due to a handicap.

1.4 Adequately providing for the dependent adult

Show the court that you are adequately providing for the dependent adult. While it is important that enough of the dependent adult's money is properly saved, it is also important that enough of it is properly spent. The judge will of course look at your accounts to see whether the dependent adult's money is likely to be enough to support the dependent adult for the rest of his or her life. However, the judge is likely to be less concerned about whether there is going to be anything left over for the dependent adult's family after his or her death.

The judge will look at expenditures for the dependent adult relative to his or her assets and income. While it is not appropriate for the dependent adult's money to be wasted, it is very much appropriate that the dependent adult receive the benefit of money he or she has earned, saved, or received during his or her lifetime. Expenses for accommodation, food, and clothing should be commensurate with the value of the dependent adult's property. Obviously where the dependent adult is wealthy, there is more available to be spent on the basic necessities. If the dependent adult can afford extras such as books, newspapers, club memberships, dining at restaurants, and travel — and is capable of enjoying those extras — then money can and should be spent on those things.

1.5 Living within the dependent adult's means

Show whether the dependent adult is living within his or her means. Realistically, living within his or her means is not always possible for a person on a fixed income and family members may be helping him or her with cash infusions or other assistance. Make sure that these cash infusions are shown on the passing of accounts under *income*.

1.6 How the assets are currently held

Show the court how the dependent adult's assets are currently held, that is, whether the dependent adult owns a house, mutual funds, or RRSP, and, if so, whose name is on the property. For example, if the dependent adult owns a house together with another person, show whether the owners are joint tenants or tenants-in-common.

1.7 Staying within the trustee's authority

Show that you stayed within the legal authority that the court granted you. This can be harder than first imagined and it is not uncommon for even the most well-intentioned trustee to make a mistake and exceed his or her authority. Exceeding your authority means using the dependent adult's money or property in ways that do not necessarily benefit the dependent adult and that are not specifically allowed by your court order. For example, you might use the dependent adult's money to give donations to charities or buy expensive birthday gifts for extended family members. If the order that appoints you as trustee does not specify that you are allowed to give away the dependent adult's money for these reasons, then you are exceeding your authority by doing so.

Another situation that arises fairly often is that the dependent adult will inherit money from a family member. Then the trustee, usually a child of the dependent adult, will divide the inherited money with his or her siblings. The theory that usually brings about this situation is that the trustee believes that one day the children of the dependent adult will inherit the money anyway so it might as well be done now. However, a trustee is not allowed to take the dependent adult's money for himself or herself, nor is the trustee allowed to give it away to people who are not dependants of the dependent adult. There is more discussion of the restrictions on trustees in Chapter 8 of this book.

If you have made an honest mistake as trustee, be straightforward with the court about it. Show the court what happened by providing paperwork and give your best explanation. Be honest about what happened and describe how you have tried to correct it. An opportunity to disclose the error and account for it is at the passing of accounts application. It is only compounding the error to allow it to carry over to a future accounting period.

2. Setting an Accounting Period

As a trustee, you will most likely pass your accounts more than once. Some trustees pass their accounts a dozen times over the years. Each time you pass your accounts, the court issues an order giving approval of the financial transactions to date. Each order covers a specific time period. You do not want the time periods to overlap. Therefore, your first task is to determine exactly the beginning and the end of the accounting period.

For your first passing of accounts, the opening day of your accounting period is the day you were appointed as trustee. You cannot choose a later or an earlier day. You are not responsible for financial transactions that happened before you were appointed, so you are not going to ask the court to approve them.

Usually, court orders that appoint a trustee will state that the trustee must pass his or her accounts by a certain day, or within a certain time period (e.g. within two years of the date of the order). That tells you the last day by which you must apply to the court. You have to allow time for your documents to be prepared, filed, and served so the accounting period must end before the court date.

For example, you may have been appointed as trustee on September 1, 2007, and your court order says that you must pass your accounts within two years. That means you must apply to the court by September 1, 2009. To give you time to get bank statements, prepare documents, file them, and serve them on various people by September 1, 2009, you will probably start getting your application ready on about July 1, 2009. Obviously your accounting period has to end no later than July 1, 2009. In this case, your first accounting period would be September 1, 2007, to June 30, 2009. Your next passing of accounts, to be done in the future, would start on July 1, 2009. Each accounting period picks up where the last one left off so there are no gaps.

3. Preparing Financial Statements in Jurisdictions Where There Are No Set Forms

Some parts of Canada require that specific forms be used for accounting. However, some jurisdictions just require that you pass accounts without rules about how those accounts must be prepared. Your checklist will specify which forms you need to use — government forms or All Jurisdictions forms.

You will note that in those jurisdictions where certain forms are required, the forms are all variations of each other. In every accounting in every jurisdiction, you are expected to start with an opening balance, add in all income, subtract all expenses, and come up with a closing balance. The closing balance must match the documentation you have from other sources such as a bank statement. Though the accounting may be lengthy and detailed, it does boil down to that simple formula. You will have to make sure that you keep records during your trusteeship that are organized and detailed enough that you can rely on them when it is time to prepare your financial statements.

4. Ledger

Keeping a daily ledger accomplishes a number of things. It keeps track of income and expenses. It keeps a running balance of the value of the property. It summarizes monthly expenses in categories such as accommodation, medical care, utilities, and food in such a way that errors can easily be noted and corrected.

A question that is frequently asked about the keeping of a daily ledger is whether a trustee needs to record every small item that the dependent adult buys on his or her own. The idea of trying to account for every cup of coffee, newspaper, package of cigarettes, or toiletry can be daunting, particularly if the trustee is not present for these purchases. A solution to this can be to provide the dependent adult with an amount of spending money that he or she can manage. This is not the solution for everyone, as each dependent adult has a unique combination of strengths and shortcomings. However, for those dependent adults who can manage small financial transactions and enjoy the freedom of doing so, giving a set amount of spending money may be the answer. It would be your job as trustee to figure out how much the dependent adult can afford to spend and how much money he or she can successfully handle and to provide that to the elderly person on a regular basis. If the amount you provide is $50 a week, your ledger would simply show an entry for $50 for "dependent adult's spending money" once a week and no further details are required. As a word of caution, excessive spending money with no explanations will likely be questioned by the court.

If the dependent adult lives in a long-term care facility, you will likely find that the facility itself is set up to handle a small amount of money on behalf of the dependent adult. It is usually called a comfort fund or trust fund and is generally not more than $200. Although the dependent adult cannot obtain cash from such a fund, he or she can charge services to it when he or she accesses those services through the facility, much as a person staying in a hotel can charge meals to his or her room. In this way, the dependent adult can have a shave, haircut, or laundry services and pay for them by way of the trust fund. You, as trustee, would replenish the trust fund as needed. Again, in your daily ledger, you need only show the expense as "long-term care facility trust fund" and you do not need to show what expenses were charged to the fund.

The CD contains a Daily Ledger form in the All Jurisdictions section that you may wish to use. You can keep the ledger on your computer, entering each item on the computer and then printing the ledger when it is finished. Alternatively, you could print out the

blank ledger and fill it in using a pen. Either method is acceptable; you should do whatever is most convenient for you.

Below you will find Sample 2, which is an example of how to use a daily ledger. Normally a ledger uses a new page for each month of the accounting period. You need to record the date of each transaction, a description, and a money amount. When it is money coming to the dependent adult, such as a pension cheque or interest earned at the bank, record it under *income*. All payments that you make or fees charged, such as bank fees, should be recorded under *expenses*.

5. Opening and Closing Inventories

As discussed in Chapter 9 of this book, as a trustee you must file an initial inventory of the property you are looking after. The inventory contains values of all of the assets. Chapter 9

Sample 2
DAILY LEDGER

Name of dependent adult: Maureen Jones

Ledger for the month of June, 2008

Item #	Date	Description	Income	Expenses
1	June 1	Old age security		
2	June 1	Accommodation		
3	June 8	Purchase of wheelchair		
4	June 15	Pension from Smith Ltd.		
5	June 21	Bank interest		
6	June 26	Spending money for dependent adult		
		Total:		

discusses the need for accuracy in the initial inventory and this section will make it even clearer why accuracy is important.

The idea of opening and closing inventories is that you have to know what you started with (an opening inventory) and what you ended with (a closing inventory). In some jurisdictions there are forms prescribed for these inventories. Obviously your opening inventory is the initial inventory that was discussed in detail in Chapter 9. Although you may not be specifically asked to file a closing inventory in all parts of Canada, you should prepare one in any event in order to pass your accounts.

To prepare a closing inventory, make a photocopy of your initial inventory. Then update the value of each asset on the inventory. For example, if the dependent adult's home was worth $200,000 when you became trustee but it is worth $250,000 now, change the value to $250,000. Do the same with bank accounts, investments, and other assets.

You will likely find that not all assets that were listed on the initial inventory are still owned by the dependent adult. For example, you might have converted an RRSP to an RRIF, sold the dependent adult's car, or put the money in a savings account into a GIC. In that case, do not list the old asset that no longer exists. Only list the new ones (e.g., the RRIF).

To your closing inventory, list any assets that the dependent adult owns now that he or she did not own when you became trustee. For example, if you have bought Canada Savings Bonds with the dependent adult's money, list those.

The date on the opening inventory was the date you became the trustee. The date on the closing inventory is the end of the accounting period that you set in section 2.

6. Summaries and Reconciliation

When passing your accounts, you need to show that you have balanced the books, just as you would balance your own chequebook. This means that you start with your opening inventory, add in all income for the accounting period, subtract all expenses, and end up with a current balance. This is a fairly simple equation in theory but can become tricky with real life numbers. If your numbers do not add up exactly, you will know that you have left something out. To balance your accounts, you need to summarize the information that appears in your daily ledger, bank statements, and any other records you have. Sample 3 is an example of the formula you will follow.

Step 1: Find your opening balance

To apply this formula to your own situation, look for the opening balance on the initial inventory you filed after you were first appointed as trustee. The net value shown on the inventory is your opening balance.

Step 2: Summarize income

Next you need to determine how much income was earned by the dependent adult in the accounting period. On the CD in the All Jurisdictions section you will find a Summary of Income form that you can print and use to help you determine the amount of income.

Sample 3
OPENING AND CLOSING BALANCE FORMULA

$125,658.32	Opening balance, i.e., value of the property when you started as trustee.
+ 37,500.00	Income from all sources during the accounting period.
- 31,869.22	All expenses during the accounting period.
= $131,289.10	Closing balance, i.e., value of the property on the last day of the accounting period.

When balancing the dependent adult's property, income will include all sources, including monthly pensions, GST rebates, occasional gifts, lottery winnings, insurance settlements, interest earned on investments, and increases in the market price of real estate. Add as many rows as you need. Sample 4 is an example of a summary of income.

Step 3: Summarize expenses

In step 3 you will determine the amount of expenses for the accounting period. This will include all monthly costs such as accommodation, food, spending money, provincial health-care premiums, medications, and clothing. It will also include occasional expenses such as purchase of a wheelchair, travel, property tax, or legal fees. On the CD in the All Jurisdictions section, use the Summary of Expenses form to help you arrive at a number. Add as many rows to the table as you need to include all of your expenses, as every case is different. See Sample 5 for an example of a summary of expenses.

Sample 4
SUMMARY OF INCOME

Summary of Income for September 1, 2007, to June 30, 2009

Income	Amount
Canada Pension Plan retirement benefit	
Old Age Security benefit	
CN pension	
GST rebates	
Interest earned	
Total:	

Sample 5
SUMMARY OF EXPENSES

Summary of Expenses for September 1, 2007, to June 30, 2009

Expenses	Amount
Accommodation (i.e., lodging, food, care, laundry)	
Transportation	
Medical expenses (e.g., wheelchair)	
Spending money ($50 per week)	
Total:	

Step 4: Reconcile

Begin with the opening balance, add in the deposits (income), and then subtract the expenses. This will leave you with a closing balance. The closing balance should match the bank statements and your other records. There is a Reconciliation of Accounts form you can use in the All Jurisdictions section on the CD. Sample 6 is an example of how to reconcile your accounts.

7. Request for Compensation

In most jurisdictions, trustees are entitled to ask the court to be paid for their time and responsibility in being the trustee. The payment comes from the dependent adult's money. As a trustee, you cannot use the dependent adult's money for your own personal gain, which means that you need court approval to pay yourself. You, as the trustee, have to initiate the question of compensation as no payment will be offered if you do not ask for it.

The time to make your request for compensation is at the passing of accounts application because the judge will have all of the dependent adult's financial information at hand. Also, the judge will be able to ask you questions about your trusteeship and how you arrived at the requested compensation amount.

As part of the order you prepare for the judge's signature, you should include a request for compensation, or a statement that you do not intend to ask for compensation. Note that there are two parts to any payment that you request for yourself. The first is the fee or wage. The second is the reimbursement for out-of-pocket expenses. You can ask for both of these parts, or just one of them, depending on your situation.

To determine how much compensation to request, see Chapter 7 of this book.

Sample 6
RECONCILE THE ACCOUNTS

Account	Amount
Opening value of the estate:	
Plus income	
Less expenses	
Plus increase in value of residence	
Closing balance of estate	
Total:	

DEATH OF THE DEPENDENT ADULT

1. Advise Public Guardian and Trustee

Regardless of which province or territory you reside in, if you are a guardian or trustee for a dependent adult who dies, you should notify the office of the Public Guardian and Trustee. There is no formal method for giving this notice. You can simply write a letter to the office identifying yourself, identifying the dependent adult who has died, and enclosing a photocopy of the death certificate. If any further information is needed, the office will ask you for it.

2. End of Guardianship and Trusteeship Order

Any court order that appoints a guardian and/or trustee automatically comes to an end when the dependent adult dies. That means that the guardian or trustee has no more authority to make any decisions for or about the dependent adult. That is now the responsibility of the executor of the dependent adult's estate. A guardian or trustee is expected to do only what is needed to account for his or her own actions to date and hand matters over to the executor.

Theoretically, the change in authority takes place the minute the dependent adult dies. In practice, however, there can be a gap of time between the death of the dependent adult and the handing over of legal authority. This happens because it takes time to transfer assets (e.g., bank accounts) from the trustee to the executor, even where there is a valid will in place, and to get the necessary paperwork done.

Where there is no will and someone has to apply to the court to become the administrator for the deceased dependent adult, the gap of time can be a number of months. This can be a tricky time for you as the trustee because your authority has come to an end but you have nobody to whom you can transfer the assets and authority. On the one hand, the law is clear that you do not have the authority to act any longer for the dependent adult but on the other hand, you cannot simply walk away leaving the dependent adult's financial matters unattended. Because you have not been officially discharged, you may still incur liability if you simply walk away without transferring assets or information to an executor.

As trustee, you will have access to all of the dependent adult's legal papers and records. On the death of the dependent adult, if you have not already done so, you should look thoroughly at the dependent adult's records to see if you can locate a will. Alternatively, you might not find a will but you might find correspondence with a lawyer or accountant that suggests where a will might be located. If you find a will or codicil among the dependent adult's papers, you should immediately contact the executor who is named in the will to ensure that he or she knows that he or she is the executor. You should also hand over to the original will to the executor. It is a bad idea to hand over an original will to members of the dependent adult's family who are not the executor named in the will as they have no legal authority to possess it or even read it, and you have an obligation to the dependent adult to protect his or her assets and privacy even after his or her death.

In British Columbia, the law specifically addresses that gap of time so that it is clear between executors and trustees who should be in charge after the dependent adult dies. In BC, the trustee is given the power to keep on dealing with the dependent adult's estate after the dependent adult dies for a limited time until a grant of probate or administration is granted and written notice of the grant is served on the trustee.

In the Northwest Territories, the gap in time is only addressed where the Public Trustee is the trustee, but not when a private individual is the trustee. Since the law there specifically states that the Public Trustee can and should carry on until a Grant of Probate is issued but does not say the same for individuals, we can logically conclude that the lawmakers did not intend for the individual trustee to have the power to continue to act until there is a Grant of Probate.

The right to make funeral or cremation arrangements for a dependent adult belongs to the executor of the estate, even if the executor is not the guardian and is not the dependent adult's next of kin. This is a long-standing right that is tied to the law of executorship, not the law of guardianship.

3. Account to the Executor

When the dependent adult has died, in most jurisdictions the trustee is required to *account to* the executor or administrator of the dependent adult's estate. This is not accounting to the court, as the executor is either a private individual or a trust company. This is an accounting only to the executor or administrator of the estate.

Accounting to the executor means providing a full explanation of all financial transactions using the dependent adult's property since the last passing of accounts at the court.

It is important to note that when you give an accounting to the executor, you still have a high standard to meet; you have to give an accounting to the satisfaction of the executor. You cannot simply hand matters over without adequate explanation, receipts, or paperwork to confirm your transactions. If the executor is not satisfied with the accounting he or she receives from you, the executor can apply to the court to compel you to give a better accounting.

As the trustee, you will be expected to hand over all books of account, ledgers, chequebooks, bank books, share certificates, bonds, deeds, credit cards, personal property, and anything else you have in your possession that belongs to the dependent adult.

If you are a trustee in this situation and you have not been paid for your services, you may wish to be paid. You should prepare a statement outlining what you are claiming for compensation. Remember to claim a wage separately from reimbursement for out of pocket expenses. Where you want to be paid a wage, give a brief explanation of how you arrived at the amount claimed. For example, if you have put in 27 hours of work for which you have not been paid, you might put on your statement that you are claiming 27 hours at a rate of $10 per hour for a total of $270. (Note this hourly rate is simply an example as there really is no going rate that can be applied right across the country.) To claim your expenses, you should attach receipts, add them all up and arrive at a total amount of out-of-pocket expenses. The statement you prepare need not be particularly formal, as long as it is clear and gives enough detail.

The statement should be given to the executor or administrator of the deceased person's estate. You will ask to be paid from the estate. This might take a few weeks or months. Your request is a legitimate debt of the dependent adult's estate so the executor or administrator is unlikely to contest it.

CHECKLISTS

The CD contains detailed checklists of the steps and forms that are needed to make an application to become appointed as guardian and/or trustee. There is a separate group of checklists for each province and territory, as the process is different in each area. Within each province and territory, if there is a different procedure for guardianship than for trusteeship, there is a separate checklist. This is not the case in every province and territory. Some checklists also include information about how to pass your accounts when the time comes, or how to apply for a review.

If you read the appropriate checklist before you start, you will get an idea of what will be required. It is a good idea to read the checklist for your province or territory through from beginning to end before you start, as you will find that certain steps can only be done if you completed earlier steps

correctly. Reading the checklist first will save you the frustration and expense of going back and repeating steps. Once you have begun your application, you can check items off to keep track of what your next step will be.

The law is always changing due to new cases being decided by the courts and new laws being passed by the government. In addition, the courts often issue practice notes or other directions to the legal profession that give instructions on how things should be done. Therefore, it is possible that the courts in your jurisdiction may have made adjustments to the procedures. Always follow specific directions that you are given by a judge, an officer of the Public Guardian and Trustee, or a Clerk of the Court.

Use the following list to choose what checklists apply to you and then go to the CD to find the appropriate checklist.

Alberta

AB1: Use this checklist if there is no guardian and you want to apply for guardianship only (no trusteeship).

AB2: Use this checklist if there is no trustee and you want to apply for trusteeship only (no guardianship).

AB3: Use this checklist if there is no guardian or trustee and you want to apply to be both guardian and trustee.

AB4: Use this checklist if you are already a court-appointed guardian (and not trustee) and you are applying for a court review of your guardianship.

AB5: Use this checklist if you are already a court-appointed trustee or you are both court-appointed guardian and trustee, and you want to apply for a review of your guardianship and trusteeship. This checklist includes the checklist for passing of trustee's accounts.

AB6: Use this checklist if you are a court-appointed trustee and you are applying only to have the court pass your accounts (no review of guardianship or trusteeship).

British Columbia

BC1: In British Columbia the roles of guardian and trustee are combined into one role known as a *Committee*. Use this checklist if there is no committee and you want to apply to be a committee to deal with personal matters, financial matters, or both.

BC2: Use this checklist if you are the committee (trustee) and you are applying only to pass your accounts.

Manitoba

MB1: Use this checklist if you are applying to be committee both of personal care and of property (same as guardian and trustee) or if you are applying just to be committee for property (same as trustee). You cannot apply to be committee of personal care only.

MB2: Use this checklist if you are the committee both of personal care and property or committee of property only and you are only applying to have the court pass your accounts (no review of guardianship or trusteeship).

New Brunswick

NB1: Use this checklist if there is currently no guardian or trustee and you want to apply to be guardian (Committee of Person), trustee (Committee of Estate), or both.

NB2: Use this checklist if you are the committee of estate or committee for both person and estate and you are applying only to have the court pass your accounts (no review of guardianship or trusteeship).

Newfoundland and Labrador

NL1: Use this checklist if there is currently no trustee (called a Guardian of Estate) and you want to apply to become the trustee (no guardianship of the person).

NL2: Use this checklist if you are currently the trustee and you wish to apply to pass accounts.

Northwest Territories

NT1: Use this checklist if there is currently no guardian and you want to apply to become the guardian only (no trustee).

NT2: Use this checklist if there is currently no trustee and you want to apply to become a trustee only (no guardianship) or if there is no guardian or trustee and you want to apply to be both guardian and trustee.

NT3: Use this checklist to apply for passing of accounts.

NT4: Use this checklist to apply for a review of guardianship o trusteeship.

Nova Scotia

NS1: Use this checklist if there is currently no guardian or trustee and you are applying to be either the Guardian of Person or the Guardian of Property, or both.

Nunavut

NU1: Use this checklist if there is currently no guardian and you want to apply to become the guardian only (no trustee).

NU2: Use this checklist if there is currently no trustee and you want to apply to become a trustee only (no guardianship) or if there is no guardian or trustee and you want to apply to be both guardian and trustee.

NU3: Use this checklist if you are trustee and wish to apply to pass accounts.

NU4: Use this checklist if you wish to apply for a review of guardianship or trusteeship.

Ontario

ON1: Use this checklist if the Public Guardian and Trustee is the guardian, and you want to apply to be appointed as Court-Appointed Guardian of the Person only (no trusteeship).

ON2: Use this checklist if currently the Public Guardian and Trustee is the trustee, and you want to apply to be appointed as Court-Appointed Guardian of Property only (no guardianship of the person).

ON3: Use this checklist if there is currently no guardian and you wish to be appointed as Court-Appointed Guardian of the Person (no trusteeship).

ON4: Use this checklist if there is currently no trustee and you wish to be appointed Guardian of Property (no guardianship).

ON5: Use this checklist if you are the court-appointed trustee and you wish to apply to pass accounts.

Prince Edward Island

PE1: Use this checklist if there is currently no guardian and you want to apply to be appointed as the guardianship of person only (no trusteeship).

PE2: Use this checklist if there is currently no trustee and you want to apply to be appointed as the trustee (known as Committee) only (no guardianship).

Saskatchewan

SK1: Use this checklist if there is currently no guardian and you are applying to become the guardian but not the property guardian.

SK2: Use this checklist if there is currently no property guardian, and you are applying either to become property guardian only, or to become both guardian and property guardian.

SK3: Use this checklist if you are a court-appointed trustee and you are applying for review of guardianship or trusteeship.

SK4: Use this checklist if you are currently property or personal and property guardian and you are filing your accounts.

Yukon

YT1: Use this checklist where there is nobody currently acting as guardian (either of the person or of his or her property) and you want to apply to be guardian of the person or of his or her property or of both.

YT2: Use this checklist to apply for a review of guardianship and trusteeship.

19

FORMS ON CD

All of the forms you will need to make your application to be appointed as guardian or trustee or both are found on or accessible from the CD that accompanies this book. There is a separate set of forms for each province and territory.

Once you have found the forms for the right geographical area, you will note that which forms are used will depend on what application you are making. For example, in some provinces the steps for applying for guardianship are different from applying for trusteeship. Applications for a review may use different forms than an initial application for someone to be appointed. Use the checklists to determine which forms you will need.

In some parts of Canada, the forms were created by the local legislatures specifically to deal with guardianship and trusteeship issues. In other areas, the forms specified are variations on standard court documents, tailored to

deal with guardianship and trusteeship issues. There are also other areas where no specific form is asked for and you are free to use any form that is comprehensive and clearly understood, within general guidelines. In this case, the forms that have been included for use are created for this book by using standard documents from each jurisdiction.

You will note that there is a section for All Jurisdictions. The forms in the All Jurisdictions section on the CD are intended to be used in situations where the law does not set down a specific form. They are in a format that is suggested rather than legislated. You may find that you do not need any of the All Jurisdictions forms if you live in a jurisdiction in which each and every form is prescribed by law. You will be able to tell which forms you need by reading your checklist. If your checklist asks you to use a specific form, you should use that one and not the All Jurisdictions form.